Nigerian Cookbook

Traditional Nigerian Recipes Made Easy

www.grizzlypublishing.com

Table of Contents

CHAPTER FOUR: NIGERIAN DESSERT RECIPES 106

CONCLUSION... 138

Introduction

First and foremost, I want to give you a massive thank you for purchasing my book, '*Nigerian Cookbook: Traditional Nigerian Recipes Made Easy.*'

Nigeria is a small country located in western Africa, surrounded by the countries of Niger in the north, Benin in the west, and Cameroon in the south east.

This incredibly unique country has a deep history, in which it has been home to a multitude of ancient indigenous kingdoms over thousands of years. As a result, Nigeria is a place that has fascinated people for the better part of a millennia.

Nigeria is a country that has an incredibly rare and varied landscape. The far south is defined by its famously tropical climate, while much of its eastern borders are typified by its rugged mountains and harsh highlands.

This clash of landscapes can be truly breathtaking at times.

When losing yourself in this amazing scenery, it is important to remember that Nigeria is also one of the most culturally deep countries on this planet. With a history that is as interesting as it is dark, Nigeria offers an isolated combination of migration and culture rarely seen – all of which has resulted in Nigeria becoming somewhat of dream location for travelers and historians alike.

When you then combine this with deep and humble people, gloriously distinctive traditions, and a very individual way of life, then you have a recipe for success.

Oh, and I should point out that the cuisine is *beyond belief.*

Like many countries found within the great continent of Africa, Nigerian cuisine is recognized by both its richness in flavor, and by its dense variety.

Over the centuries, Nigerian cooking has advanced to revolve around several unique herbs and spices, which are frequently combined with palm oil and groundnut oil to create richly flavored sauces and soups that are unlike anything else in the world.

These amazing sauces are then frequently combined with beans and legumes, as well as chicken and beef, to create some truly amazing dishes that need to be experienced firsthand to be believed.

Now, while the food is unquestionably amazing, I should really note just *how* important this cuisine is to traditional Nigerian culture. You see, over time, the local food has truly become something much greater than just *cooking*.

It has become a way of expressing Nigerian culture.

It has become a way to bring family and friends together.

In short, it has become a way of life.

In this manner, Nigerian cuisine offers an amazing collaboration between history and culture, while also providing insight into the people that inhabit this unique country.

It is truly one of the most interesting (and tasty) cuisines in the world.

So, sharpen your knives, prepare your ingredients, and light up the stovetop, because your about to take a trip to Nigeria!

Nigerian Suya Spice Mix

Yield: about 6 tablespoons

Ingredients:

- 1 table spoon sea salt
- ½ cup grounded kuli kuli (substitute roasted groundnut powder)
- ½ cup ginger powder
- ¼ cup chili powder
- ¼ cup paprika powder**
- ¼ cup onion powder
- ¼ cup garlic powder

** *Paprika powder in this context is ground dried tatashe (bell pepper), very similar to ground pepper (shombo). This helps to give the suya spice a more "Red" and bright appearance instead of the dull brown color.*

Method:

1. Combine all of the ingredients thoroughly
2. Store in an air tight container for future use

Chapter One: Nigerian Breakfast Recipes

Moi Moi (Beans Cake)

Servings: 4

Ingredients:

- 500g beans/black eyed peas
- 7 small chili pepper
- 4 fresh tomatoes
- 4 boiled eggs (optional)
- 2 ½ cooking spoons of palm oil or vegetable oil
- ½ clove garlic or ginger
- leaves, sandwich bags or aluminum cups
- cooked fish/sardines
- salt and pepper to taste
- 60g shrimps (optional)

Method:

1. First, soak the Beans/Black eyed peas for not longer than 30 – 45 minutes, wash and peel off the brown back of the beans by rubbing the beans with your palms until it becomes white then wash thoroughly. Be sure to remove all the brown peels.
2. Wash the beans till all is clean white, add onions, red chili pepper, tomatoes, chopped small garlic and a bit of ginger (very little), blend all together.
3. Boil the eggs, shrimps and fish.

4. Add 2 ½ tablespoon of palm oil or vegetable oil and seasoning like Maggi/salt then stir, taste if seasoning is okay.
5. Slice the egg and shred the fish make sure to remove the bones.
6. Rinse the leave/sandwich bag/aluminum cups, fold into a cone brake the bottom backward to avoid leakage, pour the grounded beans, add few shrimps, fresh sliced eggs and wrap the leave.
7. Put water in a cooking pan and add all the wraps inside cover to cook for 30mins.
8. Open one wrap to see if cooked and solid.

Notes:

- Instead of leaves use sandwich bags or aluminum cups.
- Make aluminum cups by cutting open cans of condensed or evaporated milk.
- Use palm oil instead of Vegetable oil with enough large red peppers to improve the richness and reddishness of moi moi, which makes it more appetizing.

Plantain Mosa (Plantain Pancake)

Servings: 6 medium pancakes

Ingredients:

- 3 tablespoons plain flour (all-purpose flour)
- 2 tablespoons evaporated milk (peak milk)
- 1 overripe plantain
- 1 large egg or 2 medium eggs
- ½ teaspoon salt
- ground cayenne pepper (to taste)
- cool water
- vegetable oil (for frying)

Method:

1. First, break the egg into a bowl, beat and set aside.
2. Peel the overripe plantain and mash with a fork till a good blend is achieved.
3. Add cool water to the mashed plantain bit by bit and mix on each occasion till you get a medium consistency.
4. Pass the medium consistency blend through a sieve into the egg. Mix very well.
5. Sift the plain flour into the mixture from Step 4. Mix thoroughly.
6. Add salt, cayenne pepper and evaporated milk and stir very well. It is ready to be fried.
7. Set your frying pan over medium heat and pour a small quantity of vegetable oil; just enough to grease the frying pan. This should be about 1 tablespoon of oil.

8. When hot, pour a small amount of batter into the pan to make a 5mm thick and 5-inch diameter plan-cake.
9. Keep an eye on it and once you see the edge of the plan-cake caking, flip it to fry the other side too.
10. It is ready when both sides are light brown.
11. Fry the rest of the dough using steps 8 to 10.

Notes:

- You need just enough vegetable oil to grease the frying pan before pouring the batter.
- You need enough water to give the mashed plantain a medium consistency so that it can pass through the sieve easily.

Nigerian Fried Plantains and Eggs

Servings: 1-2

Ingredients:

- 2 ripe plantains
- 2 large eggs or 3 medium eggs
- 1 fresh tomato
- pepper to taste
- a small onion bulb
- seasoning (as you prefer)
- salt to taste
- vegetable oil for frying

Method:

1. First, cut off the top and bottom of the plantain. Make a shallow cut on the side and peel of the skin from that point.
2. Next, cut the plantains to any shape of choice. You can sprinkle some salt on the plantain if you like salted plantains.
3. Heat up the oil and fry the plantains until brown.
4. Now chop the onions, tomato and pepper (to taste).
5. Break the eggs, add salt to taste and whisk until double in size.
6. Heat up a little oil on the pan; add the tomato, onions and pepper; stir fry for some seconds and add any seasoning of choice.
7. Next, add the whisked eggs and leave to cook for some seconds. Then turn it over, so that the other side will cook as well.

8. Now the eggs are ready to be served with the fried plantains.

Akara (Nigerian Bean Cakes)

Serves: 2-4

Ingredients:

- 2 habanero peppers (also chili peppers)
- 1 cup of beans (black-eyed or brown beans)
- 1 medium onion
- salt to taste
- vegetable oil for frying

Tools you will need:

- blender
- mortar and pestle

Before you fry akara:

- Remove the beans coat. It is important that you do not let salt come in contact with the beans you will use in making Akara till you are ready to fry it. Salt is believed to destroy the leavening property of beans. This is what prevents spattering of the beans batter during frying.
- Soak the beans in water for 2 hours to make it soft enough for your blender. If you will grind it using the heavy-duty grinders in Nigerian markets, it will not be necessary to soak the beans for extended periods of time.
- Cut the pepper and onions into desirable sizes.

Method:

1. First, grind the beans with your blender making sure you add as little water as possible. The water should be just enough to move the blades of your blender. Do not add any other ingredient when grinding the beans. It is believed that other ingredients, if added too early, reduce the ability of the ground beans particles to stick together.
2. Set some vegetable oil on the cooker to heat up. The oil should be at least 3 inches deep.
3. Put some of the ground beans into a mortar. This should be the quantity you can fry in one go.
4. Stir the beans puree with the pestle in a continuous circular motion. You need to apply some pressure so that you can energize the particles of the beans puree.
5. This stirring technique releases the gas that will act like a leavening agent to the bean's particles, making them rise and somehow stick together. This will be like the yeast making the dough rise in Puff Puff or what folding does to cake batter.
6. Keep stirring till the ground beans appears whiter and you can perceive its peculiar aroma.
7. Add some water till you get the consistency shown in the video below.
8. Check to make sure the oil is hot. The oil should be hot enough to sizzle but not too hot. If too hot, the Akara will spatter as soon as the beans batter hits the oil.
9. Once the oil is hot, add the onions and pepper to the beans puree in the mortar. Stir well.

10. Add salt to your taste and stir again. Salt should always be added just before scooping the beans mixture into the oil. If salt stays in the mixture for extended periods of time, it will destroy the leavening property of the beans. This property is what makes the Akara float in the oil and prevent spatter during frying.

11. To fry the Akara, scoop the mixture with a table spoon and slowly pour this into the oil. Dipping the spoon a little bit into the oil helps reduce spatter.

12. Fry the underside till brown and flip to fry the top side too.

13. When the Akara balls are brown all over, remove and place in a sieve lined with paper towels.

Notes:

- Use freshly peeled beans.
- Use a very small quantity of water when grinding.
- Smoothen the mix with mortar and pestle before frying.
- Add salt just before frying.

Nigerian Chicken Shawarma

Servings: 6-8

Ingredients:

- 2 chicken breasts(de-boned/boneless)
- 2 chicken thighs (de-boned/boneless), you can also use de-boned/boneless beef
- 6+ shawarma bread (either pita bread/flour tortilla wraps)
- 3 medium sized carrots (grated or cut into thin strips)
- 2 big tomatoes (cut into thin strips)
- 1 small sized cabbage (cut into thin strips)
- 1 large cucumber (cut into thin strips circles)
- 1 medium sized onion (cut into thin strips)
- 1 tablespoon vegetable /olive oil (for stir frying)
- ketchup
- mayonnaise

For the marinade:

- 2 teaspoon curry
- 1 teaspoon thyme
- 1 tablespoon vegetable /olive oil
- 1 teaspoon onion powder/2 teaspoons minced onions
- 1 teaspoon garlic powder/2 teaspoons minced garlic
- 1 large chicken stock cube/bouillon cube (crushed into powder)

- half a teaspoon black pepper
- chili pepper to taste
- salt to taste (optional)

Method:

1. Start by washing and cutting the vegetables into thin strip (if you haven't done that yet) and set aside. Also Cut the chicken or beef into thin strips and set aside. *Tip: I recommend using a combination of chicken thighs & breasts, because the fat from the thighs adds extra flavor and compliments the taste of the chicken breast.*

2. Place the chicken strips into a bowl, add the marinade and mix thoroughly until well incorporated. Then cover and store in the fridge for 2 to 24 hours (depending all how much time you have). Tip: You don't have to wait 24 hours, you can just store it overnight or for 2-3 hours, but I realized that the longer the meat marinades, the better it tastes.

3. In a pan, heat up a tablespoonful of oil. Add the marinated chicken/beef & stir fry until juicy and brown. Scoop unto a plate and set aside.

4. Mix some mayonnaise and ketchup together.

5. Place a shawarma bread on a clean flat surface and cut into two equal sizes (that's if you are using a large pita bread).

6. But if using a very flat bread or tortilla wraps, simply, spread the" mayo-ketch" on it and then fill it with the sliced vegetables on one end and sprinkle some chili pepper (optional).

7. Then fold the bread, tuck in the edge, and roll to form a shawarma wrap

Notes:

- If you want to warm it up a bit, place on a heated pan for 3 minutes (the closed edge facing the pan). If you have a microwave or sandwich maker, feel free to use those too.

Nigerian-Style Potato and Egg

Servings: 4

Ingredients:

- 5 lb. (2.2 kg) yukon gold potato (1 bag, boiled)
- 7 oz (200 g) chopped tomato
- 7 oz (200 g) baked beans (in tomato sauce)
- 4 oz (115 g) sardines
- 6 medium eggs or 5 large eggs (beaten)
- 4 tablespoons butter (cut into small pats)
- 3 tablespoons canola oil
- 1 medium onion (sliced into rings)
- 1 teaspoon garlic (minced)
- 1 teaspoon pepper
- 1 teaspoon salt
- 1 teaspoon red chili flakes

Method:

1. First, heat the oil in a medium nonstick pan over medium heat.
2. Add the onion, garlic, pepper, salt, and chili flakes, and cook for a 1-2 minutes, but don't let the onions brown.
3. Add the tomatoes, sardines, and baked beans, and cook for 4-5 minutes until the liquid reduces a bit.
4. Stir in the eggs and cook for about 2-3 minutes. Remove the pan from the heat.
5. Place a pat of butter on 3-4 potatoes, then spoon the egg mixture on top.
6. Serve hot.

Yamarita (Nigerian Egg Battered Yam Fries)

Serves: 1-2

Ingredients:

- 1-pound puna yam
- 2 large egg or 3 medium eggs
- ¾ cup all-purpose flour
- ¼ garlic powder
- ¼ curry powder
- ¼ black pepper
- ¼ thyme
- ¼ salt
- cayenne/chili pepper to your taste
- salt
- water
- a little powdered bouillon (optional)

Method:

1. Start by peeling the yam and cut into rectangles about 1 inch wide and 1/2-inch-thick and rinse and drain.
2. Put the yams inside a pot, add water about the level of the yam, also add a ½ teaspoon of salt and let it cook for about 7 minutes.
3. Drain off the excess water and transfer the yam to a bowl of cold water to stop the cooking process.
4. Once the yams are cooled drain off the water and set aside.
5. Crack the eggs in a bowl, add a pinch of salt and cayenne pepper to your taste and whisk together also set that aside.

6. In a separate bowl add the flour, garlic powder, curry powder, thyme, black pepper and bouillon and mix together.
7. Now deep the yam (one at a time if possible) in the egg and flour mixture respectively making sure the yam is well coated.
8. Heat up the oil and fry the yam turning halfway between until golden brown.
9. Serve with your favorite sauce or eat as is.

Nigerian Coconut Bread

Servings: 8

Ingredients:

- 3 ½ cups flour (plus more for kneading)
- 3 tablespoons butter or 3 tablespoons non-hydrogenated vegetable shortening (melted)
- 2 tablespoons sugar
- 1 (¼ ounce) package active dry yeast
- 1 cup coconut milk
- ¾ teaspoon salt
- ½ cup unsweetened coconut (finely grated)
- ½ cup warm water

Method:

1. First, put coconut, sugar, yeast and water into a small non-reactive bowl and stir briefly.
2. Set aside until mixture is swollen and bubbly, about 15 minutes.
3. Mix flour and salt together in a large bowl.
4. Add yeast mixture, coconut milk and butter; using your hands or a wooden spoon, stir until well combined.
5. Turn dough out onto a well-floured surface and knead, dusting with more flour as necessary, until soft and elastic, 5 to 6 minutes.
6. Form dough into a ball, dust generously all over with flour and transfer to a clean large bowl.

7. Cover bowl with a kitchen towel and set aside in a warm spot to let rise until doubled in size, about 1 ½ hours.
8. Divide dough into 8 pieces and roll each into a ball.
9. Arrange balls of dough on a large greased baking sheet, spacing them 3 to 4 inches apart.
10. Set aside in a warm spot, uncovered, to let rise until doubled in size again, about 45 minutes.
11. Preheat oven to 350°F.
12. Bake bread until deep golden brown and cooked through, 20 to 25 minutes.
13. Serve warm or set aside to let cool to room temperature.

Nigerian-Style Club Sandwich

Servings: 4

Ingredients:

- 16 slices thin white sandwich bread (crusts cut off)
- 8 slices chicken breast
- 4 canned sardine fillets
- 4 tablespoons unsalted butter (softened)
- 2 hard-boiled eggs (peeled and sliced)
- 1 small carrot (finely shredded)
- ½ plum tomato (cored, seeded and finely chopped)
- ¼ cup mayonnaise
- ¼ head green cabbage (finely shredded)
- salt and pepper

Method:

1. Mash the sardines in a small bowl with a fork.
2. Add the softened butter and mash together until smooth and well combined. Set aside.
3. Stir together the shredded cabbage, carrot, tomato, and mayonnaise in a bowl until well combined. Season to taste with salt and pepper.

To assemble:

1. Lay a piece of bread on your work surface.
2. Spread a thin layer of sardine butter over the bread, then top with 1 slice of chicken breast.

3. Top with another piece of bread, and spread some of the cabbage slaw over it.
4. Arrange a few slices of hard-boiled egg over the slaw, then top with a third slice of bread.
5. Lay 1 slice of chicken breast over the bread.
6. Spread a thin layer of sardine butter over a fourth slice of bread and lay it over the chicken, buttered-side down.
7. Repeat with the remaining ingredients to make 3 more sandwiches.
8. Cut each sandwich in half and serve.

Eggless Nigerian Pancakes

Servings: 3

Ingredients:

- 2 tablespoons butter
- 1 cup milk
- 1 or 1 cup mashed/pureed ripe banana
- ½ cup premium whole wheat flour
- ½ cup white all-purpose flour
- ¼ cup sugar
- ¼ teaspoon ground pepper
- ¼ teaspoon salt
- ¼ teaspoon nutmeg
- vegetable oil or cooking spray (for frying)

Method:

1. First, take a tablespoon of oil and add to your pan on medium heat. Spread the oil over the pan evenly. The oil is mostly to prevent sticking, so you need very little oil.
2. Once the oil is hot, use a ½ cup or any other cup you wish to pour in the pancake mix. Tilt the pan all around to spread the mix evenly.
3. Once the pancake starts cooking and coming together and you can gently get a fish slice all the way under the pancake, turn it over.

4. Keep flipping till both sides are well done. Keep the heat on low-medium heat to prevent the pancakes from burning/browning too much.
5. Repeat steps 1-4.

Nigerian Egg Stew

Servings: 5

Ingredients:

- 8 large eggs or 9 medium eggs (beaten)
- 3 tablespoons tomato paste (watered down with ½ cup of water)
- 1 habanero or scotch bonnet pepper
- 1 cup cooking oil
- 1 large onion (chopped)
- 1 stalk of spring onions (for garnishing)
- ½ green bell pepper (chopped)
- ½ red bell pepper (chopped)
- ½ tablespoon garlic (crushed)
- salt/ bouillon cube (to your taste)

Method:

1. First, heat up oil, add onions and garlic. Sauté onions and garlic till onions softens.
2. Pour in tomato paste. Fry tomato paste for about 3 mins while stirring to prevent burning.
3. Add in the chopped red and green bell peppers. Cook for another 2 minutes on low heat and it's ready to get in your belly. After cooling down to warm though.

4. Add the cup of water to the beaten eggs then gradually stir the egg/water mix into the bubbling stew. Stir continuously to break up the eggs.

5. Serve with boiled or fried plantains, boiled or fried yams, boiled or fried potatoes or a mix all three.

Nigerian Bread and Egg Casserole

Servings: 2-4

Ingredients:

- 7 large eggs or 8 medium eggs (beaten)
- 3 to 4 slices of bread
- 3 red bell pepper
- 2 stock cubes
- 1 tablespoon butter
- 1 green bell pepper
- medium sized onion
- salt to taste

Method:

1. First, chop the peppers, tomatoes, onion, and garlic. Grease an eight-inch dish with some butter and set aside
2. Sauté peppers and onions with butter for about 5 minutes. Sauté peppers and onions
3. Add the garlic, then tomatoes and the rest of the spices. Let it cook for another 3 minutes. (I added a little ugu leaves, this is totally optional). Add tomatoes and garlic
4. Tear the bread in small pieces into the casserole dish.
5. Pour in the cooked vegetables, add the eggs. Mix till ingredients are well incorporated.
6. Bake in the oven for about 20- 30 minutes.
7. Serve hot and enjoy.

Nigerian Potato Hash

Servings: 1-2

Ingredients:

- 4 medium sized red bell pepper
- 3 to 4 cloves of garlic
- 3 large potatoes
- 2 tablespoons butter
- 1 medium sized onion
- ½ teaspoon each of curry powder, ginger powder, and dried thyme leaves
- minced meat (the quantity depends on how much of it you want in your potato hash)
- salt to taste

Method:

1. First, peel and wash potatoes. Chop into bite size pieces. Also chop the peppers, onions and garlic.
2. Put the potato in a pan with cold water, add some salt, and boil for about ten minutes (don't overcook, just allow to boil till it becomes soft and the color starts to change). Drain out the water, and set aside.
3. Melt butter and sauté the peppers with onions. After about five minutes add the garlic, and all the other

spices (it is best to add the garlic after the peppers have cooked a bit, so it doesn't overcook and taste bitter).

4. Add boiled minced meat, stir together and add the potatoes. Let it cook for another ten minutes, or till the potatoes are well cooked.

5. Serve with fried egg and fresh juice. Enjoy.

Nigerian Sausage, Peppers, and Onions Bake

Servings: 1-2

Ingredients:

- 1 medium size red and green bell pepper
- sausage (whatever you like)
- onions
- salt to taste

Method:

1. Wash peppers, and take out the seeds. Peel back of onions and wash. Now chop them and put into a baking pan.
2. Add salt to the vegetables, put in the oven and let it bake for about 10 minutes.
3. Slice sausages and add to the vegetables (my vegetables were already half way cooked, if yours is raw, you may want to mix it with the vegetables at the very beginning so that everything cooks together).
4. Let it bake for another 10 minutes, be careful not to overcook the vegetables.
5. Serve hot and enjoy.

Ewa Agoyin (Boiled Beans with Pepper Sauce)

Serves: 1-2

Ingredients:

- 2 cigar cups (approx. 500g) brown/black eyed beans
- 5 cooking spoons red palm oil
- 5 big plum tomatoes
- 2 stock cubes
- 1 handful crayfish
- 1 big onion
- salt and pepper to taste

Before you cook ewa agoyin:

- Soak the beans in cold water for 5 hours. Boil the beans for 5 minutes and discard the water. Rinse the beans in cold water and set aside. This soaking and pre-cooking process will help reduce the gas inducing elements.
- Chop the onions, grind the crayfish and pound the pepper.
- Blend the tomatoes and boil the tomato puree till all the water has dried from it.
- Pre-cook the diced onions without any added water. The aim is to get it to caramelize a bit so that it will take less time to fully caramelize during frying.

Method:

1. First, cook the beans till done. For ewa agoyin, the beans need to be very soft. *(Note: if you have a pressure cooker, it is one of the staple foods you will want to use it for. It considerably reduces the cooking time.)*

2. When the beans are done, add salt, leave to dry up all the water and set aside.

3. To cook the agoyin, pour the palm oil into a separate dry pot. Allow to heat up till the oil starts smoking and the red color changes to clear. It is better to do this at medium heat so that the oil does not get too hot too quickly.

4. To keep the smoke to a minimum and still have the traditional taste of ewa agoyin, use vegetable oil and when it is very hot, add a small amount of palm oil.

5. Now add the precooked onions and stir continuously till the onions is fully caramelized. It should be very dark in color.

6. Add the parboiled tomato puree and stir continuously till you cannot tell the difference between the tomatoes and onions.

7. Add the pepper, crayfish, stock cubes and salt to taste. You can also add a little water at this point if you want.

8. Stir very well and bring to the boil.

9. Serve by dishing the beans into a plate and scoop some agoyin stew on it. Ewa agoyin can be eaten on its own, with soft and stretchy bread (known as ewa ati bread) or with fried plantains.

Bread Boat

Servings: 2-3

Ingredients:

- 5-10 baby spinach leaves
- 4 medium eggs or 3 large eggs
- 1 cooking spoon olive oil
- 1 small red onion
- 1 tablespoon diced sweet peppers (fresh paprika)
- 1 bar of baguette
- ¼ ground black pepper
- salt (to taste)

Method:

1. First, beat the eggs.
2. Add the salt, black pepper, onions and spinach. Stir very well.
3. Pour the olive oil in a frying pan and when it heats up, pour in the egg mix and spread it out.
4. After about 20 seconds, stir the egg gently. Keep stiring from time to time till the egg cakes all over. You want bold scrambled eggs.
5. Cut a long baguette bread into two.
6. Make a hole in each one like you are making a boat.
7. Fill up the hole with the scrambled eggs.
8. Serve on its own with chilled fruit juice or hot chocolate.

Notes:

- The quantities of all these ingredients can be varied to your taste and liking.
- You can use any other frying oil: sunflower oil, vegetable oils sold in Nigeria etc.
- You can use ugu instead of spinach.
- You can use tatashe instead of sweet peppers but please note that tatashe is spicy while sweet peppers are not.
- You can use an unsliced bread loaf like Agege bread instead of a baguette.

Chapter Two: Nigerian Lunch Recipes

Miyan Taushe and Tuwo Shinkafa

Servings: 1

Ingredients:

- assorted namaa (lamb chops, goat meat and cow leg)
- assorted offals (saki, fuku, heart and kidney)
- 2 pieces of scotch bonnet/habanero pepper
- 2 pieces of tomatoes
- 1 ½ cups of aborio/paella rice (for the tuwo shinkafa)
- 1 small sized pumpkin
- 1 piece of smoked fish
- 100g of sorrel leaves
- 1 bunch of spinach (spinach and sorrel leaves 2:1)
- 1 cooking spoon of palm oil (optional)
- 1 piece of red bell pepper
- 1 onion
- ½ cup of raw groundnut (you can substitute with groundnut paste)
- ¼ cup of locust beans
- seasoning cube
- salt to taste

Before cooking:

- To speed up the cooking process, do all your prepping before you start cooking. Cut the pumpkin into half, then proceed to cut into chunks. Peel the hard-outer layer, take out the seeds and the hairy pulp.

- You may be able to use canned or tinned pumpkin puree, as long as it is organic i.e. 100% pumpkin with no sugar, salt or flavoring added. If you are using pumping paste or puree, add it to the pot after the meats have cooked.

Method:

For the miyan taushe:

1. Boil and season the pumpkin with the assorted meats and smoked fish.
2. Take out the meats and fry slightly (optional), meanwhile mash the cooked pumpkin to a pulp in the pot containing the beef stock. You can choose to mash all the pumpkin chunks to a pulp or mash some whilst leaving the others in tiny bite sized pieces. Once this is done, set aside.
3. Roast the groundnut with the skin on for 3 minutes in a pan. (You can use already roasted and peeled groundnut or shop bought 100% groundnut paste). Peel the skin off, and then blend in a mill till the groundnut forms a paste.
4. Blend the ingredients for the pepper (tomatoes, onion, scotch bonnet/habanero pepper & bell pepper) and reduce it till most of the water content has evaporated.
5. Put the fried meat back into the pot containing beef stock and mashed pumpkin, let it cook till the stock starts to bubble up. Lower the heat, add the groundnut

paste, stir and let it also dissolve. You need to lower the heat to prevent the stock from thickening too fast and burning.

6. The groundnut paste will take roughly 3 minutes to dissolve thoroughly and you will notice that the stock has thickened and taken on an orange color. Add the beans and 1 ½ cooking spoons of the reduced pepper, and palm oil (if you are using). Stir and let it combine with the stock.

7. After a few minutes, the contents of the pot should look like this. Simmering nicely, you should be able to taste the groundnut and notice the difference the pepper and the beans make to the flavor profile in terms of aroma and taste.

8. This rich pumpkin soup will be watery at first. Let it sit on the heat further on low heat till it thickens, thereby intensifying the flavor. Taste for salt and seasoning cube and readjust if necessary. Wash and chop the spinach, then add to the pot.

9. Stir and let it cook for a minute or two to wilt, while it combines with the soup. Spinach is like a garnish to Miyan Taushe, i.e. the quantity to be used should not be such that the soup will resemble vegetable soup. Therefore, you need the spinach to float around in scattered pieces

10. Rinse the sorrel leaves, chop and add to the soup. The sorrel leaves truly make this dish. Sorrel has a souring, tangy taste to it which is distinct. In a few minutes after you add it to the soup, you will taste the effect. If the soup is too thick for your preference, add a little water or beef stock and you are done. The vegetables should

still be bright green, contrasting nicely with the orange of the soup, so don't cook for too long.

For the tuwo shinkafa:

1. Wash the rice with cold water, add to a pan, cover with water and cook on medium heat. If you haven't cooked with this rice before, I recommend that you add just enough water to cover the pot and monitor closely. Medium heat because you don't want the rice to burn.

2. The first stage of the cooking process, the water will be absorbed by the rice, stir and add more water, again just about enough to cover the rice. Let it cook till it becomes soggy. Try to mash the rice with the spoon and it should flatten easily. If it doesn't don't even bother trying to force it or you will become frustrated. Just add more water and repeat the process until the rice grains melt against the pot with little effort and it becomes really starchy and sticky.

3. Once you have the result that you want, lower the heat to prevent burning and proceed to folding the rice just as you would when making semovita, amala or fufu but this time mashing with a wooden spoon in the process. Make sure the heat is on low. You may need to add some more water at some point, and leave to steam. This will make the job of mashing much easier. Just don't drown it with water.

4. Keep mashing and stirring until you have a starchy rice pulp. Tuwo Shinkafa is not meant to be as smooth as semovita or poundo yam for example, so don't beat yourself up about it. You are not cooking with flour. It is meant to be slightly lumpy and grainy.

5. Serve in medium sized balls either by rolling in your hands or using a thin cellophane sheet.

Okra Soup

Servings: 2-3

Ingredients:

- 5 cups (250g) okra
- 3 cooking spoons red palm oil
- 3 stock/bouillon cubes
- 1 handful crayfish
- beef (best cut)
- iced fish (mackerel/titus), dry fish, stock fish
- pepper and salt (to taste)
- Nigerian pumpkin leaves or spinach (fresh or frozen)
- onions (optional)
- cow tripe (optional)

Method:

1. If you will use shaki (cow tripe) for the soup, wash and boil till it is done. Add water sparingly because this soup needs to be thick. Add the soaked stock fish and dry fish to the cooked shaki. The length of time it will take to cook shaki depends on the cooking appliance utilized. You can take a bite to confirm this.
2. When you are happy that the shaki and stock fish are well-done, add the beef, onions and stock cubes and cook till done. Then add the iced fish and cook till done.
3. Pour red palm oil in another pot and heat the pot to dissolve the oil if it is congealed.
4. Add the diced okra and start frying to kick-start the drawing process, add some meat stock from time to

time till you notice the okra start to draw. This process should take a maximum of 5 mins to avoid over-cooking the okra.

5. Now add the vegetable and stir well. Add all the meat and fish, crayfish, pepper and salt to taste. Then stir well.

6. Cover the cooking pot and leave to simmer and it is ready to be served.

Notes:

- Shaki, Meat, Dry Fish, Iced Fish (Mackerel/Titus) and Stock Fish must not all be used at the same time in preparing the okra soup recipe. If you can, by all means use all as they will add to the flavor. But if not, an okra soup prepared with only iced fish ((Mackerel/Titus) can equally taste good.
- Onions is optional to your taste.
- Pumpkin leaves are the best for okra soup but for those outside Nigeria, this may be hard to come by so you can use spinach. But make sure it is the washed and frozen one. This works better than the fresh and leafy spinach as far as the Okra Soup recipe is concerned.

Nigerian Honey Stir Fry Chicken Sauce

Servings: 2-3

Ingredients:

- 1 pound of chicken breast (chopped)
- 4 pieces of medium carrots (chopped)
- 4 spring onions (chopped)
- 4 cloves of garlic
- 3 tablespoons of ketchup
- 2 tablespoons of barbecue sauce
- 2 tablespoons of honey
- 2 tablespoons of butter
- 1 green bell pepper (chopped)
- 1 yellow bell pepper (chopped)
- 1 small red onion (chopped)
- 1 scotch bonnet pepper (chopped)
- 1 tablespoon of chili powder
- 1 cooking spoon of vegetable oil
- ¼ of a small cabbage (shredded)
- a small piece of ginger
- seasoning cubes

Method:

1. Start by seasoning your chopped chicken breast with the chopped scotch bonnet pepper and 1 seasoning cube and set aside.
2. Combine the ketchup, barbecue sauce, chili powder, ginger, 2 cloves of garlic, half of the chopped red onions, chicken seasoning cubes and honey in a

blender. Blend till smooth and pour over the chicken breast. Pierce the chicken breasts with a fork so the seasoning can sip through it.

3. If you have not chopped your vegetables, you can begin chopping them at this point while your chicken is marinating.

4. In a pan, pour in 1 tablespoon of butter and ½ cooking spoon of vegetable oil and allow to heat up on medium heat.

5. Once the oil is hot, toss in the remaining 2 cloves of garlic and the rest of the chopped red onions and stir fry.

6. Add all the chopped vegetables, season with seasoning cubes, stir fry for one minute and transfer into a bowl so the vegetables do not get soggy.

7. Add the rest of the butter and vegetable oil to the pan and allow to heat again.

8. Add the marinated chicken and stir fry on high heat for about 3 minutes. Reduce the heat and allow to cook. This would take 15-18 minutes depending on the size of the chicken and your cooker.

9. Taste the chicken to see if it's done and add the vegetables back to the chicken. Stir fry on high heat for 1 minute and serve with white rice, pasta or yam.

Nigerian Pork Chops and Savory Rice

Servings: 1-2

Ingredients:

- 1 pound of pork
- 4 pieces of small scotch bonnet peppers
- 4 garlic cloves
- 1 tablespoon butter
- 1 cooking spoon vegetable oil
- 1 teaspoon sugar
- 1 stalk of rosemary
- 1 teaspoon of all-purpose flour
- 1 tablespoon of lemon juice
- ½ teaspoon of black pepper
- ¼ teaspoon salt
- ¼ bulb of red onions
- a handful of yellow bell pepper (chopped)
- a handful of spring onions (chopped)
- small pieces of ginger
- seasoning cubes

Savory rice:

- 1 cup rice
- 1 cup chopped vegetables
- 1 cooking spoon vegetable oil
- 1 teaspoon lemon juice
- ¼ teaspoon black pepper
- seasoning cubes
- salt to taste

Method:

1. First, blend your ginger, 3 pieces of garlic, pepper and seasoning cubes and pour over your chopped pork pieces.
2. Add the rosemary and onions and allow to marinate for at least an hour or longer if you have time.
3. Heat up the butter and oil in a pan and chop your remaining garlic and stir fry on medium heat.
4. Add the marinated pork but not all the marinade at once and allow the pork to brown on both sides.
5. Reduce the heat to allow the pork cook.
6. Add the lemon juice, black pepper, sugar salt and if more seasoning is required, add it here.
7. Add the rest of the marinade and allow to cook. Add ½ cup of water if the pan is getting dry and one teaspoon of all-purpose flour to thicken the sauce.
8. Add the yellow bell pepper and spring onions and immediately turn off the heat so the vegetables do not become too soft.

Savory rice:

1. Wash and bring to boil one cup of rice. Season with the lemon juice, black pepper, salt and seasoning cube.
2. When the rice is soft, add the oil and stir in the chopped vegetables for 1-2 minutes.
3. Serve the rice with the pork chops.

Nigerian Salad

Servings: 1

Ingredients:

- 1 415g tin baked beans in tomato sauce
- 200g sweet corn
- 5 medium carrots
- 5 plum tomatoes
- 4 small Irish potatoes
- 3 medium eggs or 4 large eggs
- 2 medium cucumbers
- 1 medium bunch lettuce

Salad dressing:

- The classic heinz salad cream works best with this recipe. a close substitute is the heinz caesar salad cream. You can use mayonnaise too.

Before you prepare the Nigerian salad:

- Wash and cook the Irish potatoes till done. The eggs should be hard boiled. To save time, these two can be cooked in the same pot as they need almost equal amount of time to get done.
- All the vegetables need to be washed.
- Cut the lettuce into thin shreds.
- Scrape and shred the carrots using a grater.
- Peel and cut the boiled potatoes into sizeable cubes.

- Peel, remove the seeds and cut the cucumber as shown. If you want more green color in your salad, you may peel the cucumber in stripes.
- Remove the seeds from the plum tomatoes and cut into small pieces.
- Place all the cut vegetables in separate containers.
- Open the sweet corn and drain the preservation water. Rinse the seeds and set aside. Also open the baked beans tin and set aside.
- Remove the shells of the hard-boiled eggs, slice thinly and set aside. An egg slicer is perfect for this job.

Method:

1. Except the eggs, start putting the ingredients in small batches into a big salad bowl till all are exhausted.
2. Now, place the sliced eggs on the salad, covering the top.
3. Cover the bowl and place in the fridge for at least one hour. This is to allow all the ingredients to mix well.
4. Serve with a salad dressing of your choice but the heinz salad cream works best with this recipe, seconded by a caesar salad dressing.

Notes:

- If you prefer your Nigerian Salad crunchy, substitute the lettuce with cabbage. You can also use the two as the lettuce adds a green color to the salad.
- The above are the minimum ingredients for making a Nigerian salad. More ingredients such as boiled macaroni, corned beef, green bell pepper, green peas etc. can be added for varied flavor.

- The Nigerian Salad is best consumed within 24 hours of preparation if no salad dressing is added to it.
- If you are lucky to buy a baby cucumber, it may not be necessary to remove the seeds.

Egusi Soup

Servings: 1

Ingredients:

- 7– 8 cups stock
- 4 cups egusi (melon seeds, ground or milled)
- 3 tablespoons bitter leaf (washed)
- 2 teaspoons fresh locust beans
- 2 cups pumpkin leaves (cut)
- 1 cup blended onions (about 3- 5 and fresh chilies, to taste)
- 1 cup waterleaf (cut)
- ½ – 1 cup palm oil
- salt to taste
- ground crayfish to taste
- cooked meat and fish (quantity and variety to personal preference)

Method:

Egusi paste:

1. Blend egusi seeds and onion mixture. Set aside.

Make the soup:

1. First, heat the palm oil in a large pot on medium for a minute and then add the Une.
2. Slowly add the stock and set on low heat to simmer.
3. Scoop teaspoon size balls of the egusi paste mixture into the stock. Be sure to keep ball shape.

4. Leave to simmer for 20 – 30 minutes so the balls cook through.
5. Add the meat and fish and other bits which you'd like to use.
6. Add cut-up pumpkin leaves.
7. Add the waterleaf.
8. Stir and put a lid on the pot and allow cook for 7–10 minutes, till the leaves wilt.
9. Add the bitter leaf. Leave the lid off while the cooking finishes for another 5-10 minutes.
10. Stir, check seasoning and adjust accordingly.
11. Serve with white rice or yam and enjoy.

Nigerian Style Grilled Fish

Servings: 1

Ingredients:

For the fish:

- 1 teaspoon cameroon pepper
- 1 teaspoon garlic powder
- 1 teaspoon ginger powder
- 1 teaspoon onion powder
- 1 tablespoon olive oil
- 1 tilapia fish
- ½ tablespoon salt
- 1 teaspoon suya spice (optional)

For the sauce:

- 2 medium tomatoes
- 1 bell pepper
- 1 stock cube
- 1 teaspoon fresh thyme
- ½ scotch bonnet pepper
- ½ medium onion (finely chopped)
- ¼ teaspoon curry
- ¼ cup vegetable oil
- salt (to taste)

Method:

For the fish:

1. First, gut, scale and clean fish. Preset oven to 375F (~190C).
2. Combine all the spices and oil and rub over the fish on both sides. Leave to marinate for 1 hr. or overnight (preferred).
3. Place fish on a grill tray and place baking pan under tray to capture any liquid spill
4. Bake for 25 minutes then switch to broil at 525F (~275C) for 5 minutes.

For the sauce:

1. Coarsely blend tomatoes, bell pepper and scotch bonnet pepper.
2. Sauté onions in oil over medium heat then add tomato and pepper mix.
3. Season with stock cube, thyme and curry.
4. Fry for 15 minutes and taste for salt. Adjust as needed.
5. Spread some on top of fish or serve as side.

Nigerian-Style Chicken Wings

Servings: 4-6

Ingredients:

- 1 kg chicken wings, separated into flats, drumettes and wing tips (reserve wing tips for another use)
- 2-3 teaspoons dried thyme
- 2-3 tablespoons dried curry powder
- 2 -3 teaspoons chicken seasoning (or any other seasoning you like)
- 2-3 cloves garlic (without the skin)
- 2 large onions (red or white, chopped)
- 1 teaspoon smoky paprika
- ½ teaspoon turmeric powder
- fresh yellow (or red) chili (½ a chili will be a little hot, so don't use more than that if you're not a chili fan, or omit it completely)
- fresh/dried ginger (1 teaspoon, or to taste)
- salt (to taste)

Method:

1. First, blend Onions, garlic and fresh ginger, chilies, if using without water in a blender. Do it in pulses and if it is difficult, open the blender and scoop the sides in with a spatula. When ready put onion mixture into a large bowl.
2. Add spices to onion mixture and mix well.

3. Add chicken pieces to spice mixture, making sure chicken pieces are well coated. Cover the bowl with clingfilm and leave in the fridge to marinate overnight.
4. When ready to cook, put chicken and marinade in a pan and do not add any water.
5. Let steam on medium - low heat for about 15 minutes, stirring now and again so it doesn't burn. The point isn't to cook the chicken but to give the marinade one last chance to infuse the chicken with flavor. You can use the leftover cooked marinade to make stock by adding some boiling water and straining.
6. When steaming is done, put grill on medium and place chicken pieces on a baking rack and set rack about 6 inches down from the top of the grill. You may have to do this in batches. Grill to doneness and desired brownness, turning a couple of times to ensure even cooking. Alternatively, place on a baking tray in the middle of the oven set to the highest and bake/roast till done, 15 - 20 minutes.

Adalu (One Pot Beans and Corn)

Servings: 6

Ingredients:

- 1 lb./ 454 g/ 2 ¼ cup beans
- 2 medium onions (chopped)
- 1 cup sweet corn
- 1 habanero pepper (chopped)
- ½ cup palm oil
- ½ medium red bell pepper (chopped)
- ½ tablespoon sugar or sweetener of choice (optional but recommended)

Method:

1. Start by washing the beans and put in a pot with water and bring to boil.
2. Cook beans for about 30 mins then add salt/ bouillon, sugar/sweetener and half of chopped onions.
3. Cover pot and continue to cook, topping up water a little at a time until the beans is fully cooked and soft.
4. While the beans are cooking, prepare the onion-pepper medley base. Heat up the oil in a sauce pan, sauté the other half of the chopped onions, chopped pepper and red bell pepper for about 3 minutes till the ingredients are soft and tender.
5. Set aside until beans is fully cooked.
6. When the beans are fully cooked, add in the sweet corn and reduce the heat to low. Then stir in the sauce and mix until well incorporated. If the beans are dry add a

little water about ¼ of a cup allow to simmer for about a minute until some liquid bubbles to the top.

7. Stir and turn off heat. Serve warm as it is or combined with fried plantain or pap (corn pudding).

Dambu Nama (Nigerian Dried Beef Floss)

Servings: 2

Ingredients:

- ½ pound of beef
- 2 seasoning cubes
- 1 clove of garlic
- 1 tablespoon of suya spice
- 1 tablespoon of groundnut oil
- 1 teaspoon of pepper
- ½ teaspoon of chopped ginger
- pinch of salt
- handful of onions (chopped)

Method:

1. First, wash your beef and chop off the fatty parts of the meat.
2. In a pot, boil the meat with salt, pepper, onions, ginger, garlic and 1 seasoning cube.
3. Boil the beef till the water dries out and, in a mortar, pour your meat and pound.
4. If you do not have a mortar, pound the meat with your rolling pin on the chopping board.
5. Mix the beef with the suya spice and another seasoning cube in a bowl and set aside.
6. In a pan, heat up the oil but don't let it be too hot. Shallow fry the beef and strain the excess oil on a paper towel and serve with white rice.

Nigerian Goat and Spinach Stew

Servings: 2-4

Ingredients:

- 1 kg goat meat (diced)
- 20 onions (chopped)
- 1 bunch spinach (leaves only)
- 1 ladleful palm oil
- 1 ladleful dried shrimp
- chicken or beef stock
- opaki-paki spice (looks a little like a dried pod and has a mild, sweetish taste), roasted and pounded
- sunyak bah spice (like a tiny gourd - only the seeds are used. they are slightly peppery in flavour), roasted and pounded

Method:

1. First, marinate the goat meat for at least thirty minutes the opaki-paki (mild and sweet) and hot peppery sunyak bah which have been pounded in the mortar and pestle after a little roasting.
2. Fry the meat with the onions and then braise gently in the stock for about an hour or till tender. When tender,

you add palm oil and some dried ground prawns and
the spinach.

3. The palm oil has a strong red color and gives a rich,
    strong taste to the dish. Simmer for a further 20 - 30
    minutes.

4. Serve hot and enjoy.

Asa Iwa (Nigerian Cassava Porridge)

Servings: 5

Ingredients:

- 3 lbs. cassava
- 4 cloves of garlic
- 2 tablespoons vegetable oil
- 2 large red peppers (chopped)
- 1 large onion (finely chopped)
- 1 chili pepper (finely chopped)
- 1 scotch bonnet chili
- a large handful of fresh thyme
- a large knob of butter
- a large pinch of salt

Method:

1. First, peel and cut cassava, slice the pieces down the center and remove the coarse inner vein.
2. In a large heavy sauté pan heat the coconut oil, add onions, garlic, pepper, chive, thyme and vegetable oil.
3. Fry until fragrant for about 5 minutes. Add cassava.
4. Add the scotch bonnet pepper. Add butter and salt and stir.
5. Cover mixture and simmer for about 25 to 30 minutes until all the cassava is cooked and tender.
6. There should be only a small amount of coconut oil in the pan.
7. Remove the scotch bonnet chili before serving.

Nigerian Beef in Tomato Sauce

Servings: 4-6

Ingredients:

- 1 (2 lb.) new york strip steaks
- 6 chicken bouillon cubes
- 6 tomatoes
- 3 tablespoons olive oil
- 2 red peppers
- 2 onions
- 2 garlic cloves
- salt to taste
- ground black pepper

Method:

1. First, cut beef into 1 ½-inch cubes, then rinse in warm water to clean.
2. Put beef into a medium sauce pot with 1 tablespoon olive oil. Add salt and pepper, to taste, and bouillon cubes.
3. Cover and place pot over low heat. Let it steam for 20 minutes.
4. Put 3 tomatoes, 1 red pepper, 1 onion, and 1 garlic clove into a blender and pulse to coarsely chop. Then pour

tomato mixture into the pot with the beef and add the remaining 2 tablespoons of olive oil. Cook 15 minutes.

5. Stirring it on medium heat, add the remaining 3 tomatoes, cut into wedges, 1 sliced red pepper, 1 sliced onion, and 1 sliced garlic clove.

6. Cook for 15 minutes and it's ready to serve.

Seafood Jollof Rice with Pan Seared Prawns

Servings: 4

Ingredients:

- 4 tablespoons olive oil
- 4 cups water
- 2 whole habaneros
- 2 garlic cloves (minced)
- 2 tablespoons store bought seafood rub
- 2 tins tomatoes (chopped)
- 2 tablespoons salt
- 1 tablespoon tomato paste
- 1 cup long grain rice
- 1 cup green beans (top and tailed)
- 1 cup corn kernels
- 1 red pepper (sliced)
- 1 red chili
- ½ onion (sliced)
- ½ cup vegetable stock

Prawns:

- 6 medium prawns (de-shelled)
- 4 tablespoons olive oil
- 2 tablespoons salted butter
- 1 tablespoon salt
- ½ juice of lemon

Method:

1. First, cook the rice, water and salt in a medium pot over simmering temperature till rice is al dente. Cool and set aside.
2. Over high heat, sautés the onions in oil with garlic and the seafood rub till soft.
3. Reduce to medium heat and add the tomato paste followed by the chopped tomatoes. Stirring continuously.
4. Add the vegetable stock, habanero, followed by the red chili and simmer for 15 minutes.
5. Whilst simmering, in a separate pan over high heat. Flash fry the de-shelled prawns in oil and finish off with knobs of butter and a squeeze of lemon juice.
6. Lastly add the prawns, the remaining vegetables along with the rice to the pot and cook further for 4 minutes till rice and vegetables are warm.
7. Season to taste with salt and pepper.

Nigerian Kidney Bean Stew with A Peanut Sauce

Servings: 4

Ingredients:

- 1 ½ cups dried kidney beans
- 2 teaspoons salt (to taste)
- 2 tablespoons oil
- 2 garlic cloves (crushed)
- 1 cup frozen corn
- 1 small green pepper (seeded & diced)
- 1 teaspoon ground cumin
- 1 medium onion (finely chopped)
- 1 teaspoon fresh lemon juice
- ½ can (5 ½ ounce) tomato paste
- ¼ teaspoon cayenne (to taste)
- ¼ cup peanut butter (smooth is best)

Method:

1. First, soak the beans overnight. Drain. Place beans with 6 cups of water into a large pot. Bring to a boil. Reduce heat and simmer, stirring occasionally, for 2 - 2 ½ hours or until beans are tender.
2. Heat the oil in a skillet over medium heat. Add the onion, garlic and green pepper. Sauté until the onion is just translucent, turning the heat down as needed.
3. Then, add the cumin and stir once or twice. Add the tomato paste, cayenne, lemon juice and ½ cup of water. Stir and bring to a simmer. Turn the heat down and simmer for about 15 minutes.

4. In the meantime, put the peanut butter in a small bowl. Slowly add about 6 tbs of the liquid from the beans, mixing as you go. Stir this mixture back into the beans.
5. When the tomato mixture has finished cooking, pour it into the pot of beans. Add the corn. Stir and bring to a simmer. Cover, turn the heat to low and simmer gently for 10 minutes, stirring occasionally.
6. Serve hot over rice, or with a good bread.

Nigerian Chicken Stew with Okra

Servings: 6

Ingredients:

- 3 - 3 ½ lbs. chicken pieces (10 pieces)
- 1 lb. sweet potato
- 1 (15 ounce) can whole tomatoes with juice
- 1 (10 ounce) frozen okra (thawed)
- 4 garlic cloves (minced and mashed to a paste with 1 teaspoon salt)
- 2 tablespoons tomato paste
- 1 ¾ cups chicken broth (14 fl.ozs. can)
- 1 ¼ teaspoons cayenne
- 1 medium onion (chopped)
- 1 teaspoon salt
- ½ cup smooth peanut butter (at room temperature)
- ¼ cup water
- ¼ cup peanut oil or ¼ cup palm oil
- cooked rice

Method:

1. Start by arranging the chicken in 1 layer on a tray, then sprinkle with salt and let stand at room temperature 30 minutes.
2. While chicken stands, pulse tomatoes with their juice in a food processor until finely chopped.
3. Stir water into tomato paste in a small bowl until smooth.

4. Pat chicken dry. Heat oil in a 10- to 12-inch heavy skillet over moderately high heat until hot but not smoking, then brown chicken, without crowding, in 3 or 4 batches, turning over occasionally, until golden, about 6 minutes per batch. Transfer with tongs as browned to a 6- to 7-quart heavy pot.
5. Pour off all but 2 tablespoons fat from skillet, then add onion and cook over moderate heat, stirring occasionally, until edges are golden, 2 to 3 minutes.
6. Add onion, chopped tomatoes, tomato paste mixture, garlic paste, and cayenne to chicken in pot.
7. Whisk together peanut butter and 1 cup broth in a bowl until smooth, then add to chicken along with remaining ¾ cup broth, stirring to combine well (chicken will not be completely covered with liquid).
8. Bring to a boil, uncovered, then reduce heat and simmer, covered, stirring occasionally (to prevent sticking), until chicken is very tender, 25 to 30 minutes.
9. Peel sweet potato and cut into 1-inch chunks. Stir into stew along with okra, then simmer, covered, until potato is tender but not falling apart, 10 to 12 minutes.

Notes:

- Chicken stew, without sweet potato and okra, can be made 1 day ahead and cooled completely, uncovered, then chilled, covered. Reheat stew before proceeding with recipe.

Chapter Three: Nigerian Dinner Recipes

Classic Nigerian Jollof Rice

Servings: 4-6

Ingredients:

- 6 cups stock (vegetable, chicken, or beef) or water, divided
- 6 medium-sized fresh plum/roma tomatoes (chopped, or a 400-gram tin of tomatoes)
- 6 fresh, red poblano peppers (or 4 large red bell peppers), seeds discarded
- 4 cups uncooked long-grain rice (not basmati)
- 3 medium-sized red onions (1 sliced thinly, 2 roughly chopped), divided
- 3 tablespoons tomato paste
- 2 teaspoons (carribean/jamaican-style) curry powder
- 2 dried bay leaves
- 1 teaspoon (heaping) dried thyme
- 1 dash salt, to taste1 scotch bonnet peppers (to taste)
- 1/3 cup oil (vegetable/ canola/coconut, not olive oil)
- 2 teaspoons unsalted butter (optional), divided

Method:

1. First, rinse the rice to get rid of some starch then parboil: Bring the rice to a boil with 2 cups of the stock

(or water) then cook on medium heat, covered, about 12 to 15 minutes. Rice will still be hard, a bit "white" (not translucent) and only partly cooked. Remove from the heat and set aside.

2. Combine tomatoes, red poblano (or bell) peppers, chopped onions, and chili pepper in a blender; blend till smooth, about a minute or two. You should have roughly 4 cups of blended mix.

3. In a large pan, heat oil and add sliced onion. Season with a pinch of salt, stir-fry for a minute or two, then add the tomato paste, curry powder, dried thyme and bay leaves. Stir for another 2 minutes.

4. Add the blended tomato-pepper-chili mixture, stir, and set on medium heat for 10 to 12 minutes so the mix cooks and the raw taste of the tomatoes is gone. You might feel your eyes sting with onions.

5. Add 2 cups of the stock to the cooked tomato sauce, 1 teaspoon of butter, and then add the parboiled rice. Stir, cover with a double piece of foil/ baking or parchment paper and put a lid on the pan. This will seal in the steam and lock in the flavour. Cook on low heat for 15 minutes. Stir again, adjust seasoning to taste, then add the remaining 1 cup of stock. Stir, cover with foil/ baking or parchment paper and let cook for another 15 to 20 minutes, stirring every 10 minutes or so to prevent burning and till the rice is cooked and the grains are separate.

6. Don't be afraid to add some more stock or water—by the half-cup, stirring gently—if you find it a bit hard. When it's cooked, take off heat and remove the cover

of the pot. Put a tea cloth over the top and leave for half an hour or more, till ready to serve.

7. To make Party Rice, you'll need one more step. Now Party Rice is essentially Smoky Jollof Rice, traditionally cooked over an open fire. However, you can achieve the same results on the stove top. Here's how: Once the rice is cooked, turn up the heat with the lid on and leave to "burn" for 3 to 5 minutes. You'll hear the rice crackled and snap and it will smell toasted. Turn off the heat and leave with the lid on to "rest" till ready to serve. The longer the lid stays on, the smokier.

Suya (Nigerian Chicken Skewers)

Servings: 4

Ingredients:

- 1 lb. boneless skinless chicken breast
- 2 tablespoons peanuts (finely minced)
- 2 tablespoons peanut oil
- 2 tablespoons cayenne powder
- 1 tablespoon garlic powder
- 1 tablespoon ground ginger
- 1 tablespoon paprika
- 1 tablespoon dried onion flakes

Method:

1. Start by mixing all the dry ingredients together.
2. Slice the chicken into thin pieces. Sprinkle with the seasoning mix, and allow to sit for 5 minutes.
3. Thread the chicken onto skewers and brush with the oil.
4. Grill or broil for 3 minutes on each side, or until chicken is cooked through.

Notes:

- If using wooden skewers, soak them for at least half an hour before using to avoid burning.

Obe Eja Tutu (Nigerian Fresh Fish Stew)

Servings: 2-4

Ingredients:

- 1 kg fresh tomatoes or canned tomato puree
- 300g fresh fish (any fresh fish will do)
- 100g tinned tomato paste (optional)
- 1-liter vegetable oil
- 5 habanero pepper (atarodo)
- 2 or 3 medium bulbs onions
- 2 stock cubes
- thyme and curry (1 teaspoon each)
- salt to taste

Method:

1. First, blend the tomatoes, peppers and onions. If you are making use of the thick tomato paste, simply dilute it a bit in little water and set aside.
2. Pour the blended tomatoes into a pot and let it boil until the consistency is thicker and the excess water is dried up.
3. In another pot, add the cleaned cut fresh fish, add a little water, thyme, curry,1 stock cube and salt to taste. Parboil for 2 minutes, this helps to toughen the skin of the fish and get the fish tasty.
4. You can also marinate the fish with these spices overnight or for about 1 hour, if you'll rather not parboil the fish. After 2 minutes, take out the fish from the pot and reserve the liquid (fish stock).

5. Now, heat up the vegetable oil, add some onions (optional, because the blended tomatoes already have onions). Add the dried tomatoes, the diluted tinned tomatoes (derica) and fry for about 25 minutes or until the tomato loses its sour taste. Stir constantly to prevent burning at the bottom.
6. Add the fish stock and cook for 10 minutes.
7. Next, add the parboiled fish, stock cube and salt to taste. Cover and leave to simmer until the fish are properly cooked.
8. Serve with boiled rice, boiled and fried yams, plantain recipes and beans.

Notes:

- When the stew cools down a bit, scoop out the excess oil, pour into a bottle and preserve in the fridge. This fish stew oil, can be used for Nigerian soups, stew, beans recipes and yam recipes too.

Kale Jollof Spaghetti and Meatballs

Servings: 8

Ingredients:

- 1 lb. pasta of choice
- 130 g kale vegetable (chopped)
- 25 meatballs
- 4 - 6 oz (8-12 tablespoons) organic tomato paste *(see note)*
- 1 bay leaf
- 1 medium onion
- 1 teaspoon ground dry pepper
- 1 tablespoon bouillon powder
- ½ medium red bell pepper (chopped)
- ½ medium green bell pepper (chopped)
- ¼ cup cooking oil of choice (except palm oil)
- ½ tablespoon ground ginger
- ½ tablespoon ground garlic

Method:

Prepare the sauce:

1. First, heat up oil and sauté onions for about a minute.
2. Add the tomato paste and allow fry till the paste dries out but not burnt. Takes about a minute of constant stirring. Alternatively, you can dilute the paste with about a quarter cup of water and fry till all the moisture is absorbed.
3. Stir in bay leaf and spices, add 1 cup of water to the mix and then add meatballs.

4. Allow to simmer for a minute just to blend in flavors. Taste for seasoning and adjust if necessary.
5. Add the chopped green peppers and red bell peppers. Stir to incorporate.
6. Turn off heat, add the chopped kale and stir. Allow residual heat to soften the kale.
7. Set aside. and prepare the pasta.

The pasta:

1. Bring about 4 quarts (16 cups) of water to boil.
2. Add about 1 tablespoon of salt to the water.
3. Add the pasta into the boiling water and allow cook for 8 minutes I like mine al dente (not soft) if you like your pasta a little softer, then cook for about 10-12 mins
4. Turn off heat and drain the pasta with a colander reserving about 1/2 a cup of pasta water.

The mix:

1. Transfer pasta back to pot. Add the sauce and mix thoroughly. You may or may not need the pasta water to add to the moisture of the Jollof.
2. Serve and Enjoy

Notes:

- The quantity of tomato paste used depends on your choice. If you like it red, use 6 oz (12 tablespoons). If you prefer a lighter shade you use 4oz (8 tablespoons).

Nigerian Beef Stew

Servings: 6

Ingredients:

- 1 ½ lb. (680 g) flank steak (cut into strips)
- 12 oz (340 g) tomato paste
- 1 cup (240 ml) vegetable oil
- ½ cup (120 ml) water
- 6 cloves garlic
- 5 plum tomatoes (chopped, divided)
- 2 red bell peppers (chopped)
- 2 habanero peppers (chopped)
- 2 cubes beef bouillon
- 1 ½ teaspoons black pepper (divided)
- 1 tablespoon salt, plus 1 teaspoon salt (divided)
- 1 teaspoon fresh rosemary
- 1 teaspoon paprika
- 1 teaspoon curry powder
- 1 bay leaf
- ½ red onion (chopped)
- ½ red onion (sliced)
- white rice (cooked, for serving)
- fried plantain (for serving)
- scallion (for serving)
- fresh parsley (for serving)

Method:

1. Combine 4 chopped plum tomatoes, red bell peppers, chopped red onion, habanero peppers, garlic cloves,

tomato paste, 1 tablespoon salt, 1 teaspoon pepper, and water in a food processor or blender. Puree until smooth.

2. Heat vegetable oil in a large pot over medium-high heat.
3. Add the remaining tomato, sliced onion, remaining salt, and remaining pepper. Sauté until fragrant.
4. Add steak, rosemary, paprika, curry powder, and bouillon cubes. Cook until the steak is golden brown and cooked through, about 10 minutes.
5. Add the blended tomato and pepper mixture and the bay leaf.
6. Bring to a boil over high heat. Cover and simmer at low heat for 20 minutes, until the stew has thickened.
7. Fish out the bay leaf.
8. Remove stew from heat and let sit 10 minutes.
9. Serve with white rice and fried plantains. Garnish with scallions and parsley, if desired.

Nigerian Plantain and Vegetable Stew

Servings: 4-6

Ingredients:

- 1-quart broth or water
- 1-pound spinach, ugu (pumpkin) leaf, spinach or other greens (chopped)
- 6 green plantains, cut into ¼-inch thick rounds
- 3 tablespoons red palm oil or vegetable oil
- 1 onion (chopped)
- 1/3 cup ground dried crawfish or dried shrimp
- salt and pepper to taste

Method:

1. First, put the plantains, onion, dried crawfish or shrimp, broth or water and oil into a large pot and bring to a boil over medium-high flame. Reduce heat to medium low and simmer for 20 to 25 minutes, or until the plantains are nice and soft.
2. Mash the plantain a little with a potato masher to lightly thicken the stew. Stir in the spinach, ugu leaf or other greens and salt and pepper to taste. Simmer for another 5 to 10 minutes to cook the greens through.
3. Adjust seasoning and serve. Popular accompaniments include grilled or fried fish or chicken.

Variations:

- As with many stews, this recipe can be varied according to your taste and what you have on hand. Try any of the following additions:

- 1-pound chicken breast, boneless, skinless, cut into chunks
- 1-pound smoked or dried fish, cut into chunks
- 2 cups cooked black-eyed peas
- 2 cups chopped tomatoes
- Chile peppers, chopped (to your taste)
- Dried, ground crawfish is a popular flavoring in Nigerian cuisine. Dried, ground shrimp can be found in many Latin or Asian markets and is a good substitute.

Nkwobi (Nigerian Spicy Cow Foot)

Servings: 6

Ingredients:

- 2kg (4.4 lbs.) cow foot (cut into sizeable pieces)
- 20cl (200ml) palm oil
- 2 tablespoons ground crayfish
- 2 habanero peppers (or to your taste)
- 2 big stock cubes
- 1 tablespoon powdered edible potash (akanwu/kaun/keun)
- 1 teaspoon ground ehu seeds (calabash nutmeg)
- 1 medium onion
- salt (to taste)

To garnish:

- 10 Utazi leaves (Gongronema latifolium)
- 1 medium onion

Before you make the Nkwobi:

- Cut the cow foot into medium chunks. Ask your butchers cut it for you.
- Put the powdered potash into a bowl. Add a small quantity of water (about 4 table spoons) and stir well.
- Pass it through a fine sieve and set the liquid aside.
- Cut 1 onion into 4 big chunks.

- Pound the pepper with a mortar and pestle or blitz it.
- Grind the crayfish.
- Crack and remove the outer shell of the ehu then grind with a dry mill e.g. coffee grinder.

Method:

1. First, wash and put the cow foot chunks in a pot.
2. Add the stock cubes (crushed) and the chunks of onion.
3. Add a small quantity of water and start cooking at medium heat till well cooked. Add just enough water to prevent burning as you cook. There should not be any stock (water) in the pot when the meat is done.
4. While the meat is cooking, pour the palm oil into a clean dry pot.
5. Pour in the potash mixture (sieved) into the oil.
6. Stir with a wooden spatula as you pour the potash. You'll notice the palm oil begin to curdle and turn yellow.
7. Keep stirring till all the oil has turned yellow.
8. Add the ground crayfish, pepper and ehu seeds. Stir very well till they are all incorporated.
9. When the meat is done, add salt, stir and cook till all the water has dried.
10. Add the well-done cow foot to the palm oil paste and stir very well with the wooden spatula.
11. Put it back on the stove/cooker and heat till the Nkwobi is piping hot, stirring all the time to make sure it does not burn.
12. To prepare the garnish, cut the onions into rings and cut the utazi into long thin slices.

13. Serve the Nkwobi in a wooden mortar as shown in the image above.
14. Add the thin slices of utazi and onion rings on top for the full effects.
15. Best served with chilled drinks: palm wine, beer or stout and soft drinks.

Notes:

- The 2kg of cow foot may sound like a lot but, remember that cow foot is mostly bones so 2 people that love Nkwobi can finish that in no time.
- Cow foot is quite tough so if you have a pressure cooker, do use it for cooking it to save time and gas/electricity. You may be able to buy calf foot which is softer and cooks in less time.
- Ehu (Calabash Nutmeg) is a very traditional ingredient that is difficult to find outide Nigeria. If you can't buy it where you live, just prepare the Nkwobi without it. Ordinary nutmeg is not an alternative to this because they are not similar in any way. If you have friends or family in Nigeria, they will be able to buy ehu seeds and send to you, a small quantity goes a long way.
- Potash is what makes the palm oil curdle. An alternative is Ngu. It is is even more traditional than potash so if you can't find potash, chances are that you won't be able to get Ngu either.
- Utazi adds a nice bitter flavor to the Nkwobi. if you can't buy it where you live, use spinach (bold ones), it gives the same effect.

Nigerian Pepper Soup

Servings: 6-8

Ingredients:

- 1 kg chicken or cow foot or assorted beef
- 4 seeds ehu or ariwo or calabash nutmeg
- 3 stock cubes
- 2 medium onions
- 1 teaspoon of thyme (for chicken pepper soup)
- chili pepper (to taste)
- salt (to taste)
- 2 teaspoons crushed dry uziza (optional)

For grinding the ehu seeds, you will need:

- a spice/coffee grinder

Before you cook the Nigerian Pepper Soup:

- If preparing Chicken pepper Soup, it is preferable to use whole chicken instead of drumsticks. The different parts of the chicken will bring variety to the pepper soup. So, wash and cut up the whole chicken and set aside.
- If you want to prepare Assorted Beef Pepper Soup then you should buy different parts of beef - best cut, offal (shaki, round-about, liver and kidney). Wash the offal thoroughly especially the round-about which should be turned inside out during the washing. Cut these into medium pieces, just big enough to be chewed in one go.

- For Cow Foot Pepper Soup, just wash and cut the cow foot into medium pieces. In this case also, make the pieces just big enough that it can be chewed in one go. roast ehu for pepper soup
- Now it is time to prepare the 'secret' ingredient. Using an old frying pan, roast the Ehu seeds (stirring constantly) till you can smell it. Don't worry, you will know when it is OK to take it off because it has a distinctive aroma. Another way to know that it is OK is to take one of the seeds and try to remove the outer membrane. If the membrane comes off easily, then the Ehu is done. grind ehu for pepper soup
- Peel off the membrane from all the Ehu seeds and grind with a dry mill.
- Cut the onions into tiny pieces.
- Rub the dry uziza with your fingers to break them into tiny pieces.

Method:

This cooking direction describes Chicken Pepper Soup. To prepare Goat Meat Pepper Soup, Cow Foot Pepper Soup or Assorted Beef Pepper Soup just substitute chicken with cow foot or beef and offal respectively.

1. First, place the pieces of chicken in a pot and pour enough water to cover the contents of the pot. Add the stock cubes, thyme and onions and cook till done.
2. Note: When cooking Assorted Beef Pepper Soup, you should cook the shaki for some time before adding the

other beef parts. Shaki is tough and will take longer to cook than the other beef parts.

3. Cow foot is a tough part of meat so when cooking Cow Foot Pepper Soup, you should use a pressure cooker if you have one. This will save you some gas or electricity.

4. By now, you will notice that some of the water has dried. Add more water to bring it to the level of the contents of the pot.

5. Add the ground Ehu, dry uziza, chili pepper and salt to taste. Ehu has some spicy taste so you should add chili pepper with care. Even though it is called pepper soup, you still want to be able to taste and enjoy the recipe itself. Too much chili pepper will ruin it for you.

6. Cover the pot and leave to boil for 5 minutes and the pepper soup is ready.

7. Pepper Soup should always be served hot. It can be eaten alone with a chilled drink by the side. You can also eat it with Agidi, White Rice or Boiled Yam.

Isi Ewu (Spicy Goat Head)

Servings: 2-4

Ingredients:

- 1 goat head
- 15 cl (150ml) red palm oil
- 2 teaspoons ground ehu seeds (calabash nutmeg)
- 2 big beef flavored stock cubes
- 2 medium onions
- 2 habanero peppers (or to your taste)
- 1 tablespoon powdered edible potash (akanwu/kaun/keun)
- about 10 utazi leaves (gongronema latifolium)
- salt (to taste)

To garnish:

- about 10 utazi leaves (gongronema latifolium)
- 1 onion

Before you make the isi ewu:

- Cut the goat head into pieces making sure that the essential parts: ears, tongue etc. are whole cuts that is, they are not cut into pieces.
- Remove the brain and put in an aluminum foil bag then fold the bag to close.
- Wash the meat very well with foam and iron sponges where necessary, using a knife to scrape off the tough top skin especially on the tongue. There will also be traces of sooth from burning

the fur off the goat, ensure that these are all cleaned.

- Put the powdered potash into a bowl. Add a small quantity of water (about 4 table spoons) and stir well. Pass it through a fine sieve and set the liquid aside.
- Cut the 2 onions into 4 big chunks.
- Crack and remove the outer shell of the ehu then grind with a dry mill e.g. coffee grinder.
- Pound the pepper with a mortar and set aside.

Method:

1. First, cook the goat head with the chunks of onion, the stock cubes and as little water as possible. Top up the water as necessary but make sure there is as little water as possible in the pot. This is because we do not want any stock in the pot when the meat is done. Remember to cook the brain too.
2. While the meat is cooking, slice the onion for garnishing into thin rings.
3. Cut half of the utazi into thin slices. Cut the other half into tiny pieces. The first will be used for garnishing while the latter will be added into the palm oil paste.
4. When the meat is done, remove the chunks of onion, take out the brain and mash it up till smooth.
5. Add salt, stir and cook till all the water has dried.
6. Set the meat aside to cool down.
7. Now, pour the palm oil into a clean dry pot.
8. Pour in the potash mixture (sieved) into the oil.
9. Stir with a wooden spatula as you pour the potash. You'll notice the palm oil begin to curdle and turn

yellow. Keep stirring till all the oil has turned yellow. Use as little potash as possible because too much of it can upset your stomach.

10. Add the pepper, mashed brain, ehu seeds and the utazi that has been cut to tiny pieces. Stir very well till they are all incorporated.
11. Add the goat head to the palm oil paste and stir very well with a wooden spatula.
12. Put it back on the stove/cooker and heat till the Isi Ewu is piping hot.
13. Serve the Isi Ewu in a wooden mortar as shown in the image above.
14. Garnish with the thin slices of utazi and onion rings.

Notes:

- In Nigerian restaurants, the goat heads are cooked whole (without cutting them up) because they have a big pot where they can pile several goat heads and cook them at the same time.
- When preparing one goat head, it is not practical to cook it whole because you will need lots of water to get the goat head well cooked. And since we do not want lots of water in the meat when done, it is better to cut the isi ewu up before cooking it.
- Goat meat is quite tough so if you have a pressure cooker, do use it for cooking it to save time and gas/electricity.
- Ehu (Calabash Nutmeg) is a very traditional ingredient that is difficult to find outide Nigeria. If you can't buy it where you live, just prepare the Isi ewu without it. Ordinary nutmeg is not an alternative to this because

they are not similar in any way. If you have friends or family in Nigeria, they will be able to buy ehu seeds and send to you, a small quantity goes a long way.

- Potash is what makes the palm oil curdle. A healthier alternative is Ngu. It is even more traditional than potash so potash is much more available. If you can't find potash, use baking soda.
- Utazi adds a nice bitter flavour to the Isi ewu. if you can't buy it where you live, use leafy spinach (bold ones).

Afang Soup

Servings: 8

Ingredients:

- 3 lbs. goat meat (cut into large bite size cubes)
- 2 lbs. malabar spinach aka water leaf
- 57 g 2 oz dried afang leaves (may be labeled okazi/eru in the african store)
- 4 tablespoons ground smoked dried shrimp aka crayfish
- 3 teaspoons chicken bullion
- 2 red onions
- 2 scotch bonnet peppers (substitute with habanero peppers)
- ½ cup of apple snails (cooked, shelled)
- ½ clams (cooked, shelled)
- ½ cup palm oil
- 2 tablespoons cayenne pepper/ crushed red pepper flakes (optional)
- salt to taste

Method:

1. Start by slicing both onions and scotch bonnet peppers, and set them aside.
2. On low- medium heat in a large stock pot, braise the goat meat with the one of the onions, scotch bonnet peppers, 1 teaspoon bullion and 1 teaspoon salt for 30 minutes or until the meat is tender.
3. Half way into braising the goat meat, add ½ a cup of water and stir the meat to prevent in from burning.

Keep the pot covered at all times during the braising process.

4. While the meat is braising, wash your Malabar spinach in cool water to get rid of sand and dirt. Pick off the tough stems, but save the tender stems and leaves. Chop and set aside.

5. in a food processor, roughly grind the afang leaves just to break it up a little. Afang leaves are mostly sold in the African store already shredded, but you can break it up a little more using a food processor/ mortar and pestle so the shreds are not as long.

6. Once the meat is tender and is done braising. Set aside.

7. In a deep pot heat up the palm oil on medium heat (be careful not to over heat the oil on high heat) and sauté the other sliced onion for 10 minutes until it is starting to get caramelized.

8. Add in the snails and clams, and continue to sauté for another 5 minutes.

9. Add in the braise goat meat and reserve the braising liquid. It is a very flavorful stock, and will still be used.

10. Add in 2 teaspoons of bullion, crayfish, and if you are spice inclined, cayenne pepper, stir, then add in the chopped water leaf.

11. Just like regular spinach, the water leaf will look like a lot at first, but wilt down in a few minutes. once the water leaf starts to wilt, add in the Afang leaves and stir.

12. Add about 1 cup of the braising liquid to the stew, turn down the heat to low, and continue cooking with the pot covered for another 10 minutes.

13. After 10 minutes, taste the stew for seasoning and adjust the salt if necessary.
14. Turn the heat off and allow the stew to sit for 5 minutes, then serve hot

Efo Riro (Nigerian Spinach Stew)

Servings: 5

Ingredients:

- 1 lb. beef (a mixture of beef, tripe, and cow skin)
- 1 ½ pounds spinach (blanched)
- 3 large red bell peppers, 2 scotch bonnet and 1 very small onion (blended)
- 2 tablespoons crayfish blended
- 2 tablespoon locust beans
- 1 dried prawn about a handful
- 1 onion medium size (diced)
- 1 bouillon cube
- ½ cup stock fish, about 2 handfuls (shredded)
- ¼ cup palm oil

Method:

1. First, preheat the palm oil. Add the diced onion and stir-fry till golden brown.
2. Add the blended peppers and fry until the sauce thickens up.
3. Season with the stock cube, add salt to taste, crayfish and locust bean. Stir until everything is well blended.
4. Add the meat, stockfish, and dried prawns and add some water or stock to thin out the sauce, then cover it up again and allow it to come to a simmer.
5. Finally, add the spinach and mix thoroughly. Then leave it to cook uncovered for about 2 to 5 minutes. Adjust the seasoning if necessary.
6. Serve with amala, fufu, rice, or yam.

Notes:

- You can blanch the spinach before you stir them in the sauce – you can do this by adding the cut spinach in hot boiling water on a high heat, then take it off the heat immediately after it reaches its boiling point. Then pour the spinach in a sieve and rinse it under the cold water a couple of times in order to stop the cooking process.
- When frying the onions, don't leave it to burn. Once it turns a bit brown, continue with the rest of the process.
- Remember to drain off as much water as you can from the spinach. (excess water from the spinach can cause your stew to be too watery)
- You can add tomatoes if you are making a lighter version of this stew.
- If you like to use coarsely blended peppers for the stew, using a food processor rather than a blender will give you that coarse consistency.
- This stew is not a vegan stew, nonetheless, for a vegan version, you can use fried tofu or mushrooms or a combination of both.
- It's very important not to leave the spinach too long on the stove top, otherwise, the vegetables will turn brown and lose most of its nutrients in the water.

Nigerian Egusi Soup

Servings: 8

Ingredients:

- 1 lb. beef (tripe, dry fish, cow leg)
- 24 oz spinach (chopped)
- 4 tablespoons crayfish
- 3 tablespoons locust beans
- 3 cups beef stock (chicken stock works just as well)
- 2 cups melon
- 2 onions
- 1 cup palm oil (more or less depending on preference)
- 1 red bell pepper
- 1 habanero pepper
- 1 fresno pepper
- salt to taste
- stock cube (optional)

Method:

1. First, blend the peppers and onions together until smooth and set aside.
2. Blend the egusi melon, half of the second onion, and crayfish together. Set aside as well.

3. Heat the palm oil in a pan and allow it melt over a medium heat but don't overheat the oil. Add the remaining half onion (diced) and half of the locust bean. Let it cook for about 3 minutes on a medium heat.

4. Add the blended pepper and cook till the water is reduced this should take about 15 minutes on a medium heat until the water is reduced stirring about every 5 minutes to prevent burning.

5. Add the remaining locust bean, beef stock, and salt to taste. Cover and leave to cook for another 5 minutes

6. Gently introduce the blended egusi inside the sauce but don't stir it at this point. Just cover it and leave it to cook for about 20 to 30 minutes keep an eye on it so it doesn't burn but try not to stir it until the egusi turns into a soft compact mass. Then, gently stir together and add more stock or water if necessary.

7. Add the fish and meat and leave to cook again for another 5 minutes.

8. Stir in the spinach and leave to simmer for about 5 minutes (stir constantly). Adjust the seasoning if necessary.

9. Serve while still hot.

Notes:

- The typical ingredients used for egusi soup are peppers, onions, locust bean and crayfish and if you like, you can add either beef, goat meat or dry fish. Occasionally chicken and turkey are used.
- Once the egusi is well cooked, stir in the spinach. Adjust the seasoning if necessary and your egusi soup

is ready. Serve with your choice of swallow like eba, amala, semovita, pounded yam, fufu, and over rice.

- You can use tomatoes if you choose to.

Ogbono Soup and Pounded Yam

Servings: 5-7

Ingredients:

Ogbono soup:

- 1-2 pounds meat (oxtail, stew beef, tripe and cow skin)
- 3 cups chopped greens (spinach, collard greens, kale, callaloo)
- 1 tablespoon red pepper flakes
- 1 tablespoon chicken bouillon (adjust to taste bud)
- 1 cup fish (smoked)
- 1 cup onion (diced)
- ½ cup ground crayfish
- ½ cup ground ogbono
- ¼ – ⅓ cup palm oil
- salt and pepper to taste
- ½ cup ground egusi (optional)

Yam:

- 2-3 pounds African/Ghana yams

Method:

Ogbono soup:

1. Boil meat in a medium –sized saucepan, season with salt and pepper until tender (approximately 30-60

minutes depending on the choice of meat). You can shorten this process in half by using a pressure cooker.

2. Boil the cow skin and tripe together or you may do so separately until tender. Use best judgement. Remove cow skin, tripe and add to the pot of boiled meat. Add smoked fish, if using any.

3. Be sure to have enough stock from the meat (about 3-4 cups).

4. Mix ground ogbono with red oil, then add to the pot of boiled meat, followed by crayfish and scotch bonnet pepper, bring to a boil. Simmer and let it cook for about 10 minutes or more. Add chicken bouillon or cubes, if desired.

5. Add more stock water as needed to get to desired thickness.

6. Then add spinach cook for another 2-3 minutes, turn stove off and serve piping hot.

Pounded yam from scratch:

1. Peel the yam with a sharp knife, peeling away from your body carefully draw the paring knife down the body of the yam, being careful not to remove too much of the yam in during the process.

2. Look for any spoiled spots, such as bruising and discoloration in the yam as you peel. Remove the spots away with the tip of the knife.

3. Cut into large chunks and wash immediately to prevent discoloration and leave them in cool water until ready to use.

4. Add yams in a medium pot with water- enough to barely cover the yams salt to taste, if desired.

5. Boil until tender, remove from heat and immediately drain yams thoroughly in a colander. Reserve some water from the yams to use for blending.
6. Add pounded yams into food processor. Start blending then pulse every 20-30 seconds to check for smoothness. You can use a spoon to move the yam around the food processor as necessary to ensure even blending. Add about 2 tablespoons or more reserved water as needed until you achieve desired texture. Pounded yam should be stretchy and soft.
7. Wrap in a parchment paper or plastic wrap.
8. Serve with ogbono soup.

Nigerian Fried Rice

Servings: 6

Ingredients:

- 1-pound large shrimp (peeled and deveined)
- ½ pound liver (cut bite size)
- 12-16 oz vegetables (peas, carrots, green beans)
- 6 cups cooked rice (such as basmati)
- 2 teaspoons garlic (minced)
- 1 medium onion (sliced)
- 1 teaspoon white pepper
- 1 teaspoon curry powder
- 1 teaspoon pepper sauce chili sauce
- ½ teaspoon thyme
- ¼ - ½ cup canola oil
- 1-2 teaspoon maggie powder or chicken bouillon (optional)
- 1 tablespoon maggie liquid or soy sauce (optional)
- salt to taste

Method:

1. Start by breaking up the clumpy rice before starting.
2. Heat a large wok or skillet on medium high heat with about a tablespoon of canola or vegetable oil.
3. Add the rice stir vigorously for about 2-3 minutes adding Maggie liquid and a tablespoon or more of water or chicken/beef stock as need to moistened rice.

4. Set aside. Quickly wipe the wok or skillet with a clean paper towel or cloth.
5. Heat 1 teaspoon oil in the wok; add shrimp, lightly seasoned with salt. Sauté until just cooked through. Remove add to the fried rice.
6. Next add another tablespoon of oil, let it heat up, then add the liver or beef lightly season with salt and pepper, quickly stir fry for about 2 minutes.
7. Remove and add to the rice. Quickly wipe the wok or skillet with a clean paper towel or cloth.
8. Then add a tablespoon of oil into the wok, followed by onions, thyme, garlic, peas, carrots, pepper sauce, white pepper, curry powder, and chicken bouillon powder. Stir until fragrant for about 2 minutes.
9. Finally, return the combination of rice, liver, and shrimp to the wok. Stir until everything has been fully combined. Adjust seasoning salt, pepper if necessary.
10. Garnish with chopped scallion and serve.

Nigerian Chicken Curry

Servings: 8

Ingredients:

- 4 lb. (1.8 kg) boneless, skinless chicken breast, cut into 3-inch (7.5 cm) cubes
- 3 lb. (1.3 kg) red potato (quartered)
- 1 lb. (455 g) green beans (ends trimmed)
- 10 oz (285 g) frozen peas (1 bag)
- 5 tablespoons curry powder (divided)
- 4 carrots (chopped)
- 3 tablespoons olive oil
- 2 red bell peppers (chopped)
- 1 onion (finely chopped)
- 1 jalapeno (chopped)
- 1 tablespoon black pepper
- 1 tablespoon salt
- water (for boiling potatoes)
- jasmine rice (cooked, for serving)
- fresh parsley (chopped, for serving)

Method:

1. Add the potatoes in a bowl and fill with water until the potatoes are covered. Microwave on the potato setting for 10 minutes. The potatoes are done when you can pierce through them with a fork. Leave in water, and set aside until ready to use.
2. In a large pot over medium heat, add the olive oil and 3 tablespoons of curry powder, and mix thoroughly.

3. Add the cubed chicken and the onions to the pot, and mix thoroughly until chicken is cooked through, about 5 minutes.
4. Add the peas, red bell peppers, green beans, carrots, and jalapeño pepper, and mix thoroughly.
5. Add the reserved potatoes, along with 6 cups (1.4 L) of the water the potatoes were cooked in to the pot, and mix thoroughly.
6. Add the salt, pepper, and the rest of the curry powder, and mix thoroughly.
7. Bring the curry to a boil, cover, and reduce heat to low. Simmer the curry for one hour on low heat. Remove from heat.
8. Serve with jasmine rice garnished with parsley.

Chapter Four: Nigerian Dessert Recipes

Nigerian Coconut Candy

Yield: 10-12

Ingredients:

- 200g icing sugar (powdered sugar)
- 1 head fresh coconut with the juice
- water

Method:

1. First, pour the coconut juice into the pot.
2. Add the icing sugar (powdered sugar). Stir.
3. Add the tiny coconut pieces and stir.
4. Add water to the same level as the coconut pieces.
5. Cover the pot and set to boil at high heat.
6. Once the contents start boiling, stir continuously till all the water is just about evaporated.
7. Reduce to low heat and continue stirring.
8. At a time, you will notice that the contents have started sticking together. That is the sugar caramelizing.
9. Keep stirring till the coconut pieces start turning slightly brown.
10. Turn off the heat and scoop the very hot coconut candy onto a flat plate and leave to cool down.

Notes:

- Break the coconut, making sure to collect the coconut juice from it.

- Remove the meat from the shells and grate the meat into small pieces. I use the smaller openings on this grater for this task. Make sure to grate along the meat of the coconut rather than across it. This is so that you'll have long thin coconut pieces rather than a mass of grated coconut.
- The coconut candy should be sticky when cold. It should not be dry.
- You can store it in the freezer for up to a month.
- This is supposed to be a very sweet snack that is why all that sugar is used in the preparation but feel free to reduce the quantity of sugar.
- The caramel from the sugar can be tough to wash off the pot when it has cooled down. The best way to wash this off very hot water as soon as you are done with making the snack.

Shuku Shuku (Coconut Balls)

Yield: 9-12 coconut balls

Ingredients:

- 2 large egg yolk or 3 medium egg yolk
- 1 cup unsweetened flaked coconut
- 1 vanilla bean or ¼ teaspoon of nutmeg
- ½ cup flour or self-rising flour
- ¼ cup sugar

Method:

1. First, preheat oven to 375°F. Align cookie sheet with parchment or foil paper, coat with cooking spray.
2. Combine the coconut flakes, eggs, and sugar in a large mixing bowl.
3. Split open vanilla bean and scrape the inside with the dull side of a knife add it to the coconut mixture. Mix well until all the mixture is fully combined.
4. Scoop a spoonful of mixture using your hands, roll it into bite size balls. Then roll each coconut ball in flour and place on a baking sheet.
5. Bake approximately for 15 -20 minutes or until it slightly turns brown. Cool and store in an air tight container.

Puff-Puff (Deep Fried Dough)

Servings: 4

Ingredients:

- 3 ½ cups flour
- 2 cups + 1-2 tablespoons warm water
- 2 ¼ teaspoon active dry yeast (1 packet)
- ½ - ¾ cup sugar
- ½ tablespoon salt
- oil for deep frying

Method:

1. Start by mixing salt, sugar, water, and yeast. Set aside for 5 minutes.
2. Add flour and mix.
3. Let the mixture rise for approximately 1- 2 hours
4. In a large sauce pan, pour vegetable oil into a pot, until it is at least 3 inches (or about 5 centimeters) high (too little will result in flatter balls), and place on low heat.
5. Test to make sure the oil is hot enough by putting a 'drop' of batter into the oil. If it is not hot enough, the batter will stay at the bottom of the pot rather than rising to the top.
6. Using your hands grab a little bit of mixture at time and drop in the oil.
7. When the oil is hot enough, use a spoon to dish up the batter, and another spoon or spatula to drop it in the oil, sort of in the shape of a ball.
8. Fry for a few minutes until the bottom side is golden brown.

9. Turn the ball over and fry for a few more minutes until the other side is golden brown.
10. Use a large spoon or something like that to take it out of the oil. I usually place them on napkins right away to soak up some of the excess oil.
11. If desired, you can roll the finished product in table sugar or powdered sugar to make it sweeter.

Candied Peanuts

Servings: 10

Ingredients:

- 2 cups of raw or blanched or raw peanuts, almonds or cashew nuts (peeled or unpeeled works.)
- 1 cup of sugar
- ½ cup of water

Method:

1. First, pre heat oven to 275-300 degrees
2. Meanwhile, in a pot, combine the sugar and water and stir for the sugar to dissolve
3. Pour the peanuts into the sugar and water mix and stir constantly until there is no sugar syrup left and the peanuts have been completely coated. (it will look dry). This process takes about 25.30 minutes
4. Pour the now sugar-coated peanuts into an ungreased baking sheet; making sure to spread it out to prevent clumping.
5. Bake for about 25 minutes; making sure to stir constantly to prevent burning
6. Remove the baking sheet from the oven and allow for the peanuts to cool before serving.
7. Store any excess peanuts in a jar with a tight lid.

Dodo (Fried Plantains)

Servings: 6

Ingredients:

- 4 large ripe plantains (yellowish red colored)
- salt
- olive oil

Method:

1. Start by rinsing the plantains in cold water.
2. Peel them, and slice horizontally then vertically into half-moon shapes about ¾-inch wide. Sprinkle with salt, to taste.
3. Pour oil into the frying pan and heat on medium-high. When oil is hot enough, add the plantains in batches; don't overcrowd.
4. Fry plantains until golden brown. Drain on paper towels.
5. Taste and season again with salt. Repeat with remaining plantains.

Nd's Chocolate Chip Cookies

Yield: 26 cookies

Ingredients:

- 2 ¼ cups of flour
- 2 teaspoons of vanilla extract
- 2 large eggs or 3 medium eggs (room temperature)
- 1 teaspoon of baking soda
- 1 cup dark brown sugar
- ¾ cup of unsalted butter (about 12 tablespoons)
- ½-1 cup of semi-sweet chocolate chunks
- ½ cup regular white sugar
- ½ teaspoon of salt
- ¼ teaspoon of nutmeg

Method:

1. First, preheat your oven to 350 or 375 degrees.
2. Sift the flour, salt and baking soda into a bowl.
3. In a separate bowl, cream the butter and sugars. Add the eggs and mix in.
4. Add the flour, vanilla, nutmeg and the chocolate chunks. Stir until smooth. Do not over work the batter.
5. In a cookie sheet, lined with parchment paper, Drop dollops of the batter in table spoonsful. To prevent the dough from sticking, dip the spoon into lukewarm water with each scoop.

6. Bake the cookie for about 15minutes or until the rim of the cookie is a little brown. Do not overcook or let the cookie over brown.

Chin Chin

Servings: 10

Ingredients:

- 280 g / 13/4 cup all-purpose flour
- 82 g / 1/3 cup granulated sugar
- 57 g / 4 tablespoons salted butter
- 1 large egg or 2 medium eggs
- ½ teaspoon baking powder
- ½ teaspoon ground nutmeg
- ¼ cup evaporated milk
- oil for deep frying

Method:

1. First, measure and Mix dry ingredients in a bowl and set aside.
2. Measure and mix wet ingredients together except butter.
3. Add butter to the dry ingredients and mix with your fingers until just combined.
4. Pour in the other wet ingredients and mix together until dough forms. it should form a perfect dough but if it feels a bit stiff, add a Tbsp of water or milk. if it feels too tacky, add a Tbsp or 2 of flour no more. DO NOT over work the dough.
5. Wrap in a saran wrap and allow to rest on the counter for about 5 mins. this allows flavors blend in and develops the gluten which makes it easier during the cutting process

6. Unwrap rested dough, you can roll out all the dough at once since dough is small or you can divide into 2 portions and roll individually. Roll out dough to about a quarter of an inch thick because dough will rise when you fry them.
7. With a knife or pizza cutter or even a dough divider cut dough across vertically and horizontally forming little squares.
8. Put little squares in a bowl and sprinkle a little flour on them and shake to prevent sticking.
9. Heat up oil. Fry till light golden. Remove with a slotted spoon and spread on a paper towel lined tray to cool. Chin chin will be soft when hot but hardens as it cools.

Nigerian Fruit Salad

Servings: 10-12

Ingredients:

- 4 ripe papayas or 4 mangoes (peeled, seeded and cut into bite-size pieces)
- 2 red apples (cored and chopped)
- 2 ripe bananas (peeled and sliced)
- 1 (16 ounce) can pineapple tidbits (well-drained)
- 1 cup fresh orange juice
- 1 tablespoon granulated sugar
- ½ teaspoon ground cinnamon
- 1/3 cup sweetened flaked coconut

Method:

1. Combine papayas, apples, bananas, pineapple, orange juice, sugar, and cinnamon in large bowl. Toss to mix well. Cover and chill until ready to serve.
2. To serve, sprinkle with shredded coconut.

Caramelized Bananas

Servings: 4

Ingredients:

- 16 ounces brown sugar
- 8 ounces whipped cream
- 1 bunch banana
- 1 cup butter

Method:

1. Start by peeling all bananas and after doing so split down the middle and then cut in half, optional to cut in half but you do need to split, it is easier on me to quarter them and makes a good presentation.
2. Place cut bananas aside and melt 1 stick of butter, set the other stick aside in case you need more when cooking, if you use a lot when dredging the bananas then you will need to melt before starting to fry.
3. Once butter is melted start warming your skillet on medium high, watch closely as you will only want to slightly brown when cooking so it won't take long.
4. While skillet is heating up please take your bananas and start buttering both sides of each slice very well. Use a brush to do so or you can dredge them through the butter if you wish but please keep in mind doing so will soak up more butter so please be careful if you do not wish them buttery.
5. After all slices are done add butter in the skillet (enough to coat the bottom well).

6. Then start placing slices in the skillet, when you have a skillet full take brown sugar and start adding, no measurement is needed as you just cover them.

7. After you coat a side with brown sugar on the first coat flip them over and coat the next side and let them sit for about one minute.

8. After the minute is up flip and coat again as doing so add brown sugar in the pan and let it cook along with the rest, it does not have to be a lot but I judge it by the way people like caramel, so please just try a little at first as this is very rich.

9. When bananas are golden and slightly brown down the center they are done.

10. Remove from skillet and place on plate. Add whip cream to top and serve hot.

11. Then repeat until you finish.

Nigerian Mango & Banana Sundae

Servings: 4

Ingredients:

- 4 tablespoons orange juice
- 4 scoops vanilla ice cream
- 2 bananas
- 2 tablespoons lemon juice
- 1 mango, fresh (or canned)

Method:

1. First, peel the mango if using a fresh one & finely chop. Peel the bananas & slice finely in rounds.
2. Put the fruit into a large bowl. Add lemon and orange juice. Toss lightly.
3. Place one scoop of ice cream in a sundae dish. Cover with ¼ of the mixed fruit & repeat with the remaining ice cream & fruit.

Agbalumo Ice-cream Cake

Yield: 1 cake (2-4 servings)

Ingredients:

- 3-4 agbalumo fruits (peel the skin and finely chop the flesh. carefully remove the seeds and use as part of your garnish)
- 2 oreo biscuits (crushed, remove the cream from the biscuit, alternatively use any of your preferred biscuits)
- 1 large tub vanilla ice-cream
- chin-chin (crushed, optional)
- roasted ground nuts/peanuts (crushed, optional)
- honey or cane sugar syrup (you can also use more healthy alternatives like maple syrup or agave nectar)

Method:

1. First, prepare the fruit well in advance of making your ice-cream cake. In a small container, add some syrup to the chopped agbalumo. Add as much or as little syrup as you wish. The more syrup the sweeter and mellower the taste. Allow this to marinate for at least 6 hours or overnight. The longer the better.
2. Remove the ice-cream from the freezer and allow to stand for a short while to melt a little. When melted enough to incorporate other ingredients, transfer into a mixing bowl and add the crushed biscuits, chin-chin and peanuts (if using). Also add a good portion of the

syrup marinated agbalumo. (Save some to serve with the ice-cream cake later).

3. Mix well for an even distribution of all ingredients.
4. Line any available bowl, cake pan or jelly mold, with some cling film (or food grade cellophane wrap). This will facilitate easy removal of the frozen ice-cream cake.
5. Transfer the ice-cream mixture into the lined bowl. Gently tap the bowl on the table to level the mixture, and remove any air bubbles trapped in.
6. Place the bowl into the freezer and allow to freeze preferably overnight.
7. Serve with the remaining syrup marinated agbalumo with the whole cluster of seeds.

Notes:

- Some of the ingredients have no specific reference to quantity, to enable you to adjust them to meet your preference for sweetness, textures and flavors.

Kunun Gyada (Groundnut Milk and Rice Gruel)

Servings: 1-2

Ingredients:

- 600 ml cool water
- 150g raw groundnuts (peanuts)
- 50g soft rice variety
- tamarind (tsamiya) to your taste

Before you make kunun gyada:

- Soak the rice for at least 8 hours.
- Soak the raw groundnuts (peanuts) for 3 hours.
- Soak the tamarind in warm water till soft and extract the juice as shown in the video below. Set aside.
- When soaked, blend the groundnuts with 400 ml of water and extract the groundnut milk as detailed in the Groundnut Milk recipe.
- Blend the rice with 200 ml of water and set aside.

Method:

1. First, pour the groundnut milk into a pot and start cooking on medium heat. Stir it all the time so that it does not stick to the bottom of the pots. Lumps will also form if you do not stir it often.
2. When it boils, slowly add the rice blend while stirring at the same time.
3. When it boils again, add the tamarind juice.
4. Keep stirring and once it heats up again, it is ready to be served.

5. Serve Kunun Gyada hot/warm with Akara (Kosai) or drink on its own as a comfort drink.

Notes:

- You must use RAW groundnuts (peanuts) for Kunun Gyada.
- You can buy tamarind and raw groundnuts from African and South American food shops all over the world.
- Use the soft variety of rice.
- Add tamarind to your taste.

Kankaran Tsamiya (Frozen Tamarind Juice)

Yield: depending on the quantity

Ingredients:

- tamarind (tsamiya)
- lukewarm water

You will also need:

- A container for freezing them. You can also use transparent plastic bags.
- A fine sieve
- A freezer

Method:

1. First, peel and soak the tamarinds in lukewarm water.
2. When soft, mash them up or rub in a sieve till you get a smooth puree. For best extraction, remove the seeds from the tamarind before soaking them.
3. Pour the mashed mixture through a fine sieve.
4. Pour the extract into containers and place in the freezer overnight.
5. When completely frozen, remove from the ice cube trays and lick immediately.

Mingau de Tapioca (Nigerian Tapioca Pudding)

Servings: 6-8

Ingredients:

- 4 cups water
- 2 cups coconut milk
- ½ cup tapioca granules (or pearled tapioca)
- ½ teaspoon ground cloves (or to taste)
- pinch of dried, crushed bay leaf (optional)
- pinch of salt
- sweetener (sugar, honey, agave nectar, etc.), to taste
- freshly grated nutmeg (to taste)
- coconut cream, condensed milk, fruit jams, sauces, toasted nuts or cereal, to serve, whatever you like.

Method:

1. First, soak tapioca in the coconut milk and 2 cups of water for an hour or two at room temperature so the granules absorb the liquid and soften
2. In a pot or pan, combine soaked tapioca, ground cloves, cinnamon powder, bay leaf if using and a pinch of salt
3. Cook on medium to low heat about 15 - 20 minutes, stirring with a (large) whisk so the tapioca doesn't clump up, cooks evenly and the bottom doesn't burn.
4. Add a cup of water and cook till the tapioca swells, some granules become translucent and soften. Add the second cup of water so the resulting consistency is

liquid, of single cream consistency. Add more water if needed to keep the consistency liquid.

5. Once cooked through, sweeten to taste.

6. Serve warm with a sprinkling of freshly, finely grated nutmeg. Add the toppings you like, whether it's fruit jams or toasted nuts.

7. Leftover tapioca pudding keeps well in the fridge. The granules firm up and gel/jelly more. To reheat, add milk to taste and reheat gently on the stove.

Pawpaw (Papaya Cake)

Servings: 2-4

Ingredients:

- 175g plain flour (sift to aerate)
- 175g of unsalted butter
- 120g of caster sugar
- 100g of very ripe, peeled and diced pawpaw (papaya) *(note: ensure that the pawpaw is a ripe one)*
- 2 tablespoons of fresh milk or evaporated milk
- 2 large eggs or 3 medium eggs
- 1 teaspoon of baking powder

Method:

1. First, pre heat oven to 180 C.
2. Pour the diced pawpaw into a small sauce pan, add two spoons of sugar, about a cup of water and boil for about 3 minutes under low heat.
3. Allow to simmer until it reduces into a syrupy mass. Set aside to cool.
4. Then begin to make the cake batter by mixing butter and sugar together in a bowl until fluffy.
5. Whisk the eggs and add to the mixture. Mix well.
6. Mix the baking powder into the flour and gently add them to the mixture. Mix batter well with a wooden spoon.
7. Add the pawpaw jam/syrup and the milk. Mix well until you achieve a batter that drops/flows easily when

lifted with a spoon. Ensure the pawpaw is well distributed within the batter.

8. Transfer batter into a baking pan and bake for 25/30 minutes or until cake is cooked through. Use the toothpick test to check when the cake is cooked. The tooth pick must come out clean when pierced into the cake. *Note: this cake is a little dense, so once baked, remove from baking pan and allow to cool (otherwise it may become soggy).*

Nigerian Pound Cake

Servings: 30 (makes 3 loaf pans)

Ingredients:

- 500 g butter /margarine
- 480 g of all-purpose flour
- 400g- 450g granulated sugar
- 10 large eggs or 12 medium eggs
- 2 ½ teaspoons baking powder
- 2 teaspoon pure vanilla extract
- ½ teaspoon ground nutmeg (optional)

What you will need:

- 3 loaf pans or 1 round 8" pan + 1 loaf pan
- food scale
- stand mixer or hand mixer. (you can still bake without these but it's harder)
- an oven

You can still bake even if you don't have an oven. You can simply use a stove, a pot big enough to contain the cake pan, some sharp sand, three flat topped stones to create a tripod effect and foil.

Method:

1. First, preheat the oven to 350°F/180°C
2. Measure out all your ingredients.
3. Sieve the flour, baking powder and nutmeg into a bowl and set aside.

4. Crack the eggs and beat them, then add your pure vanilla extract to the beaten eggs

5. Prepare your pans with baking spray or by greasing with butter/ shortening and flouring them or you use homemade goop

6. In a Stand mixer with the paddle attachment, mix the butter and sugar for about 5 mins till it becomes fluffy and lighter in color. See picture below for how the appearance progresses to fluffy

7. Add your beaten eggs and the flour in three parts alternating the eggs and flour starting with the eggs and ending with the flour. (Which means you add a third of the eggs, mix then you add a third of the flour mix again until the flour is just incorporated. Continue in this pattern till you have mixed in all the beaten eggs and flour)

8. When you have mixed in all the eggs and flour then mix up the batter for another minute and it is ready. (The batter should drop from your spoon when lifted up but not runny.)

9. Pour into prepared pans and bake in the middle rack of your oven at 350*F for about 45 - 50 minutes or until you insert a toothpick and it comes out clean.

10. When this yummy creation is ready, bring it out of the oven, allow to cool in the pan for about 5 mins then place on a cooling rack to cool completely.

11. Enjoy plain with warm milk, hot chocolate, ice cream and berries or caramel topping. Your options are endless

Notes:

- It is best to Preheat your oven at the right time which is as stated above just before you start measuring out your ingredients.
- When you put the cake in the oven DO NOT open the oven before 30mins. In fact, it is best not to open the oven at all until close to the end of its baking time say 40mins.
- Start checking for doneness at least 10mins before the stated time. First thing you should do before pricking it with a tooth pick is to touch the top with your fingers and press it lightly if it bounces back then it is done. You can now double check by inserting the tooth pick or skewer.
- When mixing in the flour, mix until just incorporated means * * until the flour mixes in not necessarily completely don't over mix because it will develop the gluten in the flour which results in a tough dense chewy texture which is not what we a looking for in a yummy fluffy cake is it? gluten is good for breads and maybe cookies but not cakes.

Beju

Yield: 20 cookies

Ingredients:

- ½ lb. fresh grated coconut (about 1 coconut), or dried shredded coconut
- ½ lb. cassava root
- ½ cup sugar

Method:

1. First, peel the cassava root and grate it. It is also possible to grate the cassava in the food processor but the result might be a little coarser.
2. Place the grated cassava root in a cheesecloth and squeeze out the excess moisture and starch from the cassava.
3. Grate the coconut or shred it in the food processor. It is also possible to use dried shredded coconut.
4. For this recipe, it is preferable to use caster sugar (finer than regular sugar) but crystal sugar will also work.
5. Mix the three ingredients in a bowl.
6. Preheat oven to 300 F.
7. Meanwhile, pour a little of the mixture into muffin molds. You can also use rings and pack the preparation within the rings.
8. Place in the oven. After 20 minutes, turn the biscuits over and cook for another 10 minutes.
9. Take the cookies out of the oven and sprinkle them with icing sugar (optional).

Nigerian Meat Pie

Servings: 10 pies

Ingredients:

For the dough:

- 1kg (8 cups) plain flour (all-purpose flour)
- 500g (1.1 lbs.) margarine
- 2 teaspoons baking powder
- 2 pinches salt
- ½ cup / 125 ml / 4.2 oz cold water

For the filling:

- 500g (1.1 lbs.) meat (minced)
- 2 medium Irish potatoes
- 2 medium carrots
- 2 cooking spoons vegetable oil
- 2 knorr cubes
- 2 tablespoons plain flour
- 1 medium onion
- 1 teaspoon thyme
- 1 cup / 250 ml / 8.4 oz cold water
- salt to taste

Other:

- 1 medium egg

Method:

For the filling:

1. First, peel the Irish potatoes and scrape the carrots, wash and cut these two into tiny cubes.
2. Wash and slice the onions into tiny pieces.
3. With your cooker or stove set to medium heat, heat the vegetable oil in a pot, add the diced onions and stir for a bit, add the minced meat and stir vigorously till the minced meat turns pale.
4. Add 1 cup of water, Knorr cubes and thyme. Cover the pot and once the contents of the pot start boiling, add the diced carrots and potatoes and cook till everything is well done.
5. Dissolve 2 tablespoons of plain flour in half cup of cold water and add to the meat pie filling. This tip is so that the meat pie filling does not dry up during baking. It is also what keeps the meat pie filling moist.
6. Add salt to taste, stir the contents and turn off the heat. Set the meat pie filling aside. Now is the time to prepare the dough for the meat pie.

For the dough:

1. Put the 1 kg of flour in a sizeable bowl; add 2 teaspoons of baking powder and 2 pinches of salt. You really do not need a lot of salt for the meat pie dough. The meat pie will get most of its taste from the filling. Mix these dry ingredients very well.
2. Use a tablespoon to scoop the margarine in small bits into the bowl of flour. The smaller you make the bits of margarine, the easier it will be for you to rub them into the flour.
3. Use finger tips to rub the margarine into the flour till the mix becomes like crumbs. *Note: In Nigeria, we*

refer to margarine as butter but for my audience in the Western countries, please do NOT use butter for the meat pie dough because butter is too hard and this makes it difficult for you to mix it with the flour to achieve the crumbly look. So please use margarine. Also, butter is quite heavy so it makes the dough very greasy which hinders the elasticity of the dough.

4. Start adding cold water in bits while at the same time folding the mix till a stiff ball of dough is formed. You will be surprised at how small quantity of water you need to get the dough stiff. At most, all you need for the 1 kg of flour is half a cup of water.

5. Knead the dough very well, put back in the bowl and leave to rest for 5 to 7 minutes. This makes the dough more elastic.

Cut, fill, fold and close:

1. Set your oven to 170°C (335°F) and leave to preheat while you continue with the meat pie.

2. Rub margarine on the insides of the oven tray and set aside. This is so that the undersides of the meat pies do not burn or stick to the tray during baking.

3. Break the egg, beat it and set aside, you will need it pretty soon.

4. Knead the dough some more, roll it out to achieve a 5mm thickness.

5. Use a cutter, be it the cover of a small pot or a meat pie cutter, to make round cuts on the rolled-out dough.

6. Remove the excess dough, leaving behind the round cuts.

7. Scoop some meat pie filling into the center of the round cuts, the quantity should be such that you can comfortably close the dough without overflows.
8. Don't worry if you over-filled the first one, you have many meat pies to fill today so at some point you will know just the right quantity of meat pie filling to scoop into the dough.
9. Rub the egg on the inside edge of the cut meat pie dough. This is to ensure that your meat pie is perfectly sealed and does not open up while it is being baked.
10. Fold one part of the dough to meet the other end and use a fork to press the 2 edges together to close tightly.
11. Place your work of art in the oven tray and repeat the previous step till all the cut-out dough is exhausted.
12. Roll out more dough, cut, fill, close and place in the greased oven tray till all the dough is used.
13. Rub the egg on the meat pies. This gives the meat pie a golden-brown look when done.
14. Set the tray in the preheated oven and bake for 30 to 40 minutes. This time will depend on the type and heating capacity of your oven. The important thing to know is that the best meat pies are the ones baked at medium heat. You can confirm that the meat pie is done when it starts browning. It is alright to open the oven to check this.

Conclusion

Once again, I would like to thank you for purchasing my book.

You now have everything you need to consistently produce traditional Nigerian meals suitable for absolutely any occasion. With dishes for breakfast, lunch, dinner, and desert, you can not only experience every aspect of Nigerian cooking, but also share it with your friends and family, just as they do in Nigeria

Just keep in mind that to truly become a good cook you must constantly work towards it. To bring out the flavors of each ingredient, you have to practice, sharpen your skills, and refine your personal taste.

So, take the time to trial every recipe in this book. Slowly and surely you will enter the heart of Nigerian cooking, and experience some of the best flavors on the planet in the process.

And of course, make sure that you enjoy the process!

Other Books by Grizzly Publishing

"Jamaican Cookbook: Traditional Jamaican Recipes Made Easy"

https://www.amazon.com/dp/B07B68KL8D

"Brazilian Instant Pot Cookbook: Delicious Pressure Cooked Meals Made Fast and Easy"

https://www.amazon.com/dp/B078XBYP89

"Norwegian Cookbook: Traditional Scandinavian Recipes Made Easy"

https://www.amazon.com/dp/B079M2W223

"Casserole Cookbook: Delicious Casserole Recipes From Around The World"

https://www.amazon.com/dp/B07B6GV61Q